Rudy Duran

"WARNING"

This book contains material not appropriate for those under 18. It is R-rated for language, profanity, adult content, violence, trauma, disturbing images, depression, sexuality, sexual situations, and mature subject matter.

READER DISCRETION IS STRONGLY ADVISED

Cover Designer: Chamika Dinesh
Front Cover Photographers: Verdi Photography & Sound Design L.L.C , Rudy Duran
Trauma Body Art: Ebony.Jonelle
Interior Photography: Rudy Duran, Verdi Photography & Sound Design L.L.C, 3KP Marketing, JAMEEL DAVIS, JP Films, Author NeeNee Marie, Jedi Arts, Tyrone Willis, Jessica Bacon, Excellence Noir, Jaheir Davis
Models: Author NeeNee Marie, Tiffany W., Jaheir D., Jason D., Brea L., Kiara, Kevin C., Octavia H., Faith S., Shraina D.,

Interior Graphic Designer and Photo Editor: Kensho
Back Cover Photography: JAMEEL DAVIS
Page Designer: Chamara Cruzz (cruzz creation)

Editor: KYA PUBLISHING CANADA
Publisher: ELEVATEDWAVES PUBLISHING CORP.
(Garfield Heights, Ohio)

ISBN-13 (Paperback): 978-1-7331082-6-3
ISBN-13 (Hardback): 978-1-7331082-7-0
ISBN-13 (ebook): 978-1-7331082-4-9

Library of Congress Control Number: 2020949060

First Edition

Printed in the United States of America

Davis' books may be purchased in bulk for promotional, educational, or business use. Please contact your local bookseller or ElevatedWaves Publishing at ElevatedWavesPublishing@gmail.com

For more information regarding publicly for author interviews, email Jameel Davis at jdavi122@kent.edu

COMPLETELY NAKED

by
JAMEEL DAVIS

FOREWORD BY
HENRY FORD
&
STACEY MARIE ROBINSON

There are times when I SCREAM IN SILENCE,
Hoping Someone Could Hear Me, So I Can be RESCUED from this
HOSTAGE SITUATION.

CAN ANYONE HEAR ME?

Jedi Arts

I DO NOT WANT TO FALL VICTIM TO THE BULLET!

There are parts of this world that are beautiful, and there are many beautiful people in it. But those beautiful parts and people are constantly being destroyed by capitalists and communists, removing my safe haven, and forcing me to fall prey to predators.

PLEASE CAN WE HAVE OUR FORESTS BACK?
CAN I PLEASE BE RELEASED BACK INTO MY NATURAL HABITAT

Dedication
Acknowledgments
Foreword
Introduction

Remarks from the Author
Tears of A Hummingbird
Plan of Action

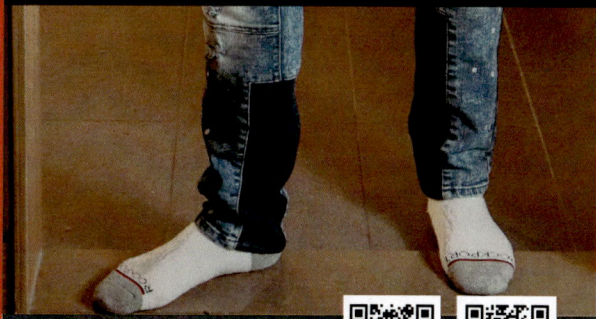

Behind the design

DEDICATION

This body of work is dedicated to the many people who will soon be inspired by my anatomy and physiology: 206 bones, over 600 muscles, and my 11 organ systems including my circulatory, respiratory, digestive, excretory, nervous, and endocrine systems, my immune, integumentary, skeletal, muscle, and reproductive systems that all functioned together to build the guts and courage to reveal my naked self herein to the world.

If you are looking to put a halt to the vicious cycle of psychic trauma in which you have been the perpetrator and/or the victim, and wish to begin your healing process so you can become better and encourage and help your family and others become better, then this book is for you.

ACKNOWLEDGEMENTS

I would like to thank myself for having the mindset, discipline, and courage to sit and write this very moving book in just 19 days, and for being brave enough to allow the world into my vault I once had password protected. This puts me at book four. I would like to thank my amazing editor, writing and cultural friend, Stacey Marie Robinson of Kya Publishing, for investing in me as a person and in my writing career. Stacey, thank you for trusting me with enhancing your vision for your movement in Toronto, Ontario and for assisting me with taking my talents to another level. You really helped bring this book to life and I could have not trusted another person or company with my manuscript.

I would like to thank my fun, passionate, all-around amazing street team members: Octavia, Jessica and Tonisha, for their feedback during the creation of this book, for investing into my books; leaving reviews, posing for cool photos and videos with my books, and helping me spread the word about my books and events to others. I am truly grateful for them.

I would like to thank the many people who have grown to love me over the years through my writings, teachings, personality and as a man — my family, countless of friends, fans, students and colleagues.

Lastly, I would like to thank you for purchasing your copy of Completely Naked which has helped keep my career as an author afloat. Please share this book with a friend, colleague, family member, or a person in need.

Henry Ford:

When Jameel Davis invited me to write the Foreword for Completely Naked, the only letters I could locate on my keyboard were "Y", "E", "S". He had just handed me a ticket to climb aboard a fast-moving express train that was destined for greatness. This young, dynamic, powerful international author only travels first-class, yet he remains grateful to all who helped fuel his journey.

From the moment I read the warning message, "This book contains . . .," I realized I was about to enter uncharted territory. As an author of six motivational self-help books, and a veteran of thirty years sharing empowerment from the pen and the podium, all my warnings are safe for the eyes and ears of the most sheltered. Jameel is not that restrained, and for good reason. He promised to become unclothed, and he fulfilled his promise. His masterful use of words, and the fearlessness of using some raw ones, entice the reader to keep the book open long past sleep time. His message reveals many of his innermost thoughts and reflections. Jameel's responses to those thoughts and reflections, are the seeds that provided his growth and maturity; that in turn, offer you a bountiful harvest.

Completely Naked takes you on a journey of amazing heights, but also through valleys of despair. In this journey called life, we all seek safe travel and rewarding destinations. We want the comfort and the view, but we fear the valleys and protest the rough side of the mountain. Jameel takes the reader on the complete trip. Completely Naked examines obvious and subtle ways our development and behavior can be impacted by others. The book reveals how persuasive outside pressures can be, whether caused by parental absence or dysfunction, or the temptation to follow the so-called norms of society. Often, the pressures have roots that began over 400 years in the past, where the forced landing of Blacks on the American continent, created conditions that predictably programmed us for failure. Jameel's ability to connect the dots that far back are testament to his amazing insight, reflection, and the growth he has experienced.

The lessons available from the author's 'undressing' include the revelation that, "we can grow through what we go through." Living in an age of information abundance, we are blessed with the ability to learn from someone else's mistakes, begin healing from someone else's injuries, and start our climb of the mountain from someone else's 'base camp'. We can avoid some of the roadblocks, flatten some of the steep inclines, and speed our journey to greater rewards and completeness by reading Completely Naked — reflecting upon its messages, objectively considering our own behavior, and working toward becoming whole.

God has blessed us greatly by introducing us to Jameel Davis and Completely Naked.

I believe that consistency is key when it comes to giving advice—solicited, or otherwise. Consistency in behaviour, and transparency in experience. When you seek words of leadership from a trustworthy source, you want to know that at the root of their advice is a lived experience. Something authentic. I had the honour of editing Jameel Davis' book "Completely Naked," and was truly captivated from beginning to end. Not only because of the extreme vulnerability and personal anecdotes that Jameel sacrificed in creating this project, but also because of the power of his words and the great potential his stories had to heal any engaged reader of his text. Jameel is wise far beyond his years. He has a heart of gold, a spine of steel, and he is clearly committed to taking each and every lesson and blessing in his life and sharing it with his community.

He has been given the gift of language and an engaging character: his books have given him the privilege of influence that will allow him to be used as a tool for progress, enlightenment, and success. As a reader, a friend, as a public figure, and as a Black man, Jameel's experiences are brilliantly recalled. Sometimes painfully so.

The story unfolds in a way that readers of all ages and life circumstances can walk away from "Completely Naked" feeling as though they have learned something new about life, about the author, and most importantly, about themselves. Congratulations to Jameel on creating yet another significant piece of writing, and special thanks to him for having the bravery to reveal his soul in pages of this book.

About Stacey M. Robinson

Writing The Black Narrative // How To Tell Your Cultural Story

In Between These Sheets Book Review

Cultivating Minds To Own Thyself Book Review

Recap: KYA Publishing and ElevatedWaves Publishing Writing Workshop

INTRODUCTION

Why Completely Naked?

There are hidden layers beneath me I have yet to reveal to the world, not in my previous published works or vocally in front of an audience. At the age of thirty (10-26-2019), I felt the urge to unveil those hidden layers—the edgier and more emotional side of me. A side of me that I had locked away, deep into the abyss from the public, my family, and even my best friends. Although I have been healed for quite some time now, I have kept this part of me away because the timing to share it with the world was not right. I needed time to gather my thoughts and figure out the best possible way to approach my audience with the information I had password protected. The time has come for me to let you into my vault.

Completely Naked, is a look at people of color in our unnatural (broken) state, in which our brokenness affects our relationships with each other and our ability to live dignified and wealthy lives. It is a look at assisting those of us who are battling demons and traumas with finding our inner voices so we can share our darkness out loud, which can guide us on the road to recovery, finding our true self and inner peace.

Not only is this book intended to help people of color reveal our skeletons in order to heal, but it is also intended for people of other ethnic backgrounds to examine their behaviors and history of psychic trauma as well, so they can begin to heal and move forward properly.

Many of us are angry with ourselves and one another, and don't know the real reasons why; it is not our fault. You will soon find out why many of us are hurting inside, who caused us the pain we are experiencing, and ways we can heal, as I begin to undress myself and the subjects herein with complete vulnerability.

Please Proceed Forward
With Caution.

You May not Like it,
You May Even be
Afraid to do so,
But, You Must Undress
Yourself too.

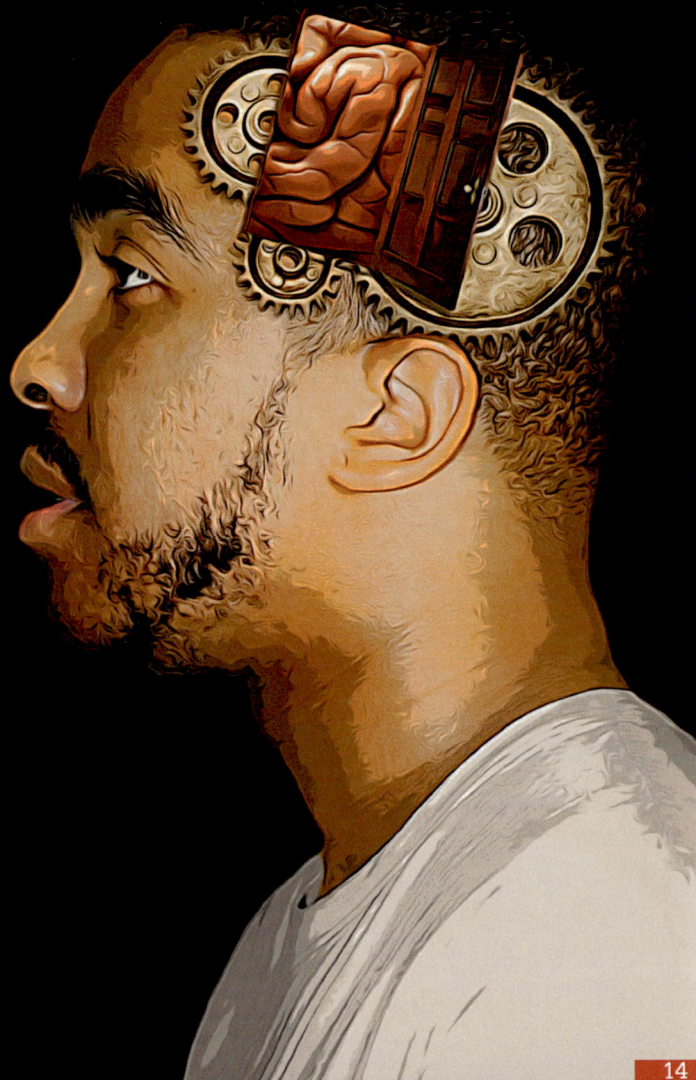

COME ON IN

I AM GETTING

NAKED

Author NeeNee Marie

EVEN WITH YOUR CLOTHES ALL OFF, YOU'RE STILL NOT NAKED!

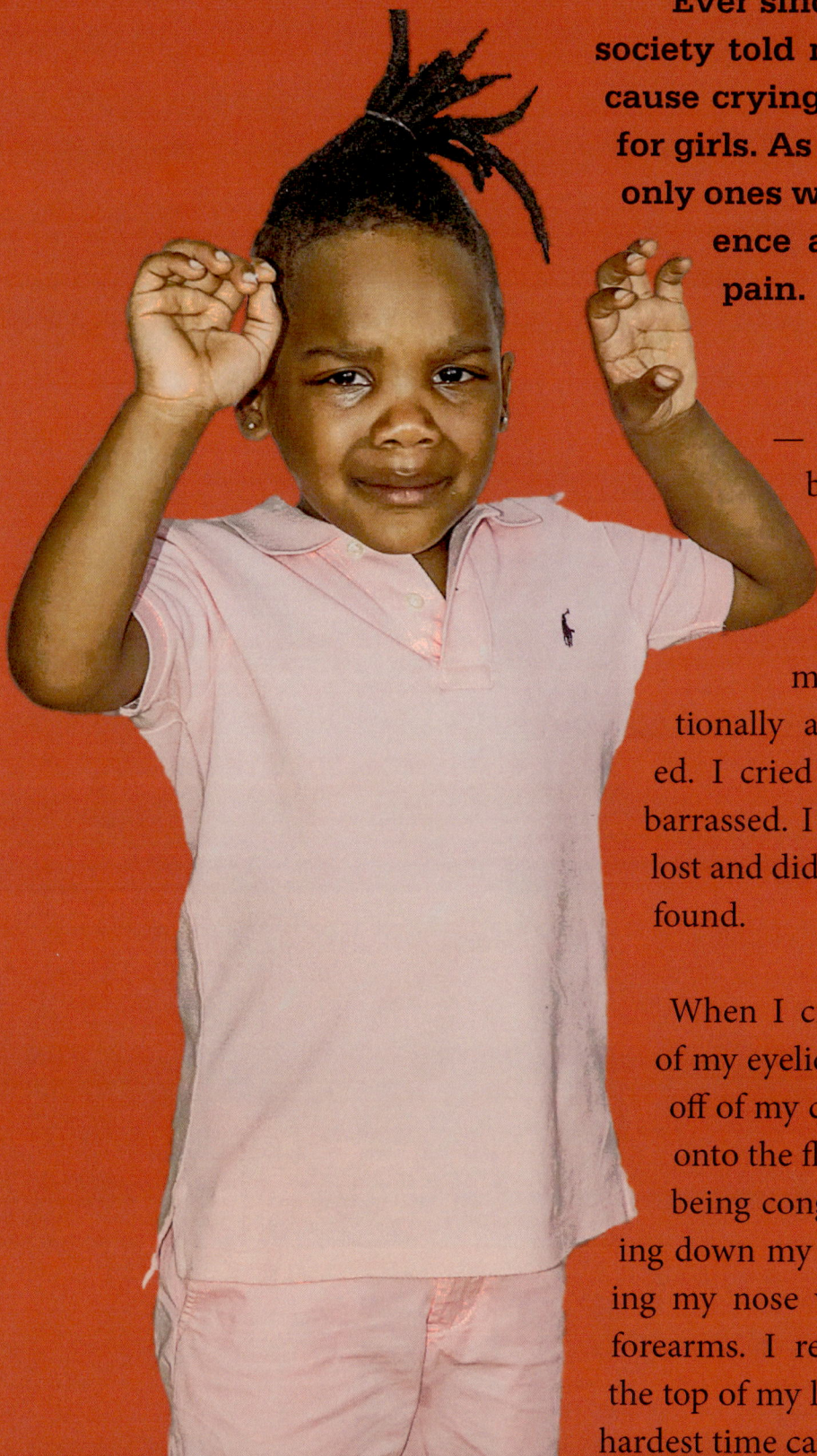

Ever since I was a toddler, society told me to not cry because crying is for sissies. It's for girls. As if females are the only ones who should experience and express their pain.

But, I cried anyway — until I was forced to become mute.

I cried because I was physically, mentally and emotionally abused and neglected. I cried because I was embarrassed. I cried because I was lost and did not know how to be found.

When I cried, tears raced off of my eyelids, down my cheeks, off of my chin, to my shirt and onto the floor. I recall my nose being congested and snot racing down my lips, each time wiping my nose with my hands and forearms. I remember wailing at the top of my lungs and having the hardest time catching my breath.

I remember being left alone until my tears and snot ran its course; no arms to comfort me or lips to ask me what was wrong. No words of encouragement to help me fight through the physical, mental, and emotional pain I was experiencing.

I was Just left with dried up snot, tears and crumpled up tissue paper.

I remember crying my eyes out, only able to see the color red, as my head pounded and pounded as if I was being beaten with a hammer — from migraines that seemed to never go away.

I remember being in a room hours at a time, screaming at the top of my lungs before being taken to the emergency room. I remember the pain in my head alleviating each time I arrived at the emergency room entrance. I remember doctors not being able to find a cure. I remember being neglected, yelled and screamed at, and each time my severe migraines would return. All because I was expressing out loud how bad I was suffering severely inside, and there was nothing I could do about it.

"Shut the fuck up."
"Stop crying like a girl."
"Shut your cry-baby ass up."
"Stop crying like a Bitch".
"Shut your whining ass up,"

As I continued and repeatedly balled my eyes out.

I remember being threatened with more harm if I didn't stop crying.

"Shut the fuck up, before I give you something to cry about."

So, I listened. I decided to be quiet because...

"Boys Don't Cry."
"Boys Don't Cry."
"Boys Don't Cry."
I had to just Man Up!

18

I had terminated my freedom of speech and expression, causing me to self-destruct; all because society had programmed me to believe, "if I showed any sign of emotion, I am weak and less of a man."

Why does society get to decide who I am before I'm even able to speak?

Here is a look at me in a way you have never seen me before: Completely Naked.

Fasten your seatbelt as I take you on a long, mind-blowing adventure on the non-magic school bus through my mind, veins, nervous system, beneath my layers of skin, tendons, and muscles, undressing my complete skeletal system. On this journey,

you will discover parts of me and even parts of yourself that many people especially men keep locked away. If exposed, it could possibly lead to a life of public humiliation and embar-rassment, which could possibly make you feel less of yourself if your truth ever got out.

This gut-wrenching unmagical adventure is Intense, Sensitive, Uncomfortable, Amusing, and Unforgettable. It's a journey for those who are brave. Hold On Tight!

01 CHAPTER ONE

"I CHEATED"

Behind The Design

JP Films

WHO EVER TOLD YOU TO STAY AFTER THEY HAVE HURT YOU, **FUCK THEM!**

No one should ever have to endure pain from someone who is supposed to love and protect them, and one should not be encouraged to return back to the ones who have intentionally and unintentionally caused them great pain, especially when the person(s) who caused them pain have not corrected their behavior.

Why encourage a person to return to their abuser? Why encourage them to stay, and risk getting hurt over and over again?

FUCK THAT! That shit does not feel good. It does NOT feel good at all.

And, fuck the part of the wedding vows that says: "...or for worse...'till death do us part."

The problem I have with that part of the vow is that it encourages spouses who become victims to abuse, to endure pain until either they or their spouse is removed from this earth. It is one of the most uncomfortable phrases I have ever heard from a spiritual doctrine, and one of the many reasons why I entirely reject religious leaders who join man and woman together with that vow.

If I were to get married, how do they have my marriage in their best interest if they are asking me if I vow to stay with this woman during my worst until we are separated by death? I have heard many people say to me: "not that kind of worse," and I have replied: "how do you measure worse?" And I was left without a response. Let's take a look at the meaning of the word worse: a more serious or unpleasant event or situation (morally wrong, corrupt, frightful, depraved, awful, miserable, painful, all things that aren't good).

Why would a leader of a spiritual institution, or those who advocate for a religious text, encourage someone to stay in a terrible situation? A situation that could cost them their life? So they can get some of the insurance money? I believe any book, doctrine, pastor, or person that instructs you to remain with someone who abuses you should be dismissed from your life, and you should ask for your money back if you paid someone to marry you using the "...or for worse...'till death do us part" vows because they did not have your best interest nor safety at heart. I believe they just wanted your money. I recommend re-newing your vows with new and healthy phrases, if your marriage is healthy. One should not adopt something that encourages you to stay in an abusive marriage.

IF YOU ARE IN AN ABUSIVE-MARRIAGE, GET OUT NOW!

Those of you who are in an abusive and controlling relationship, the moment you see an opportunity to leave, run away and never look back; I don't care how good the sex is, how much money they have or how much you think you need them, Just GO! Your life and happiness are much more important. Do not tell your partner that you are leaving. Just GO! Verbal abuse leads to physical abuse and if you choose to stay through it, you are damaging and crippling yourself even more; one day, you may not wake up because you decided to stay.

Do not believe them when they say they are not going to harm you anymore. If they did it once, more than likely they will hurt you again.

You deserve to be Protected, Happy, and Cherished; not to be living in fear or with pain inside of a home with someone who lacks emotional and self-control: someone with mommy, daddy and psych issues.

I once lacked emotional and self-control, which caused many of the females I dated in my adolescent and young adult years great heartache and pain. If you are one of those women and you are reading this, I openly apologize for the pain I caused you, and even though I am apologizing now, I am not asking you to be in my presence once more. I understand firsthand how the smallest thing can trigger an abused person. **So yeah, fuck me too for the pain I caused you, because I should have had parents who taught me the proper way to treat and to protect a woman,** instead of pouring my mommy and daddy issues on you in the form of verbal, mental, physical, and emotional abuse. I should have been taught to heal and find self-love first before I started dating and/or having sex with you.

I am no longer a person who makes up excuses for my behavior, but a person who now owns up to my wrong doings; I have self-accountability. As I mentioned before, I have emotionally scarred women I have been involved with, and it was before I had self-control, before I became aware of myself, my childhood traumas and triggers, and before I became a man. I did not become a man until I was twenty-six years old.

Some of my behaviors toward the women I dated and had sexual relations with was a result of childhood abuse, neglect, molestation, and having a lack of self-control. My lack of self-control was due to not having someone teach me self-discipline and how to manage my emotions of pain and frustration. As a result of not being properly taught, I kept a lot of my pain and frustrations bottled up inside because I was programmed to never show a sign of emotion, which kept me from finding personal happiness and maintaining a healthy relationship with the women I had been involved with.

By not having a positive outlet to release my built-up anger, it was only a matter of time before I exploded. When the temperature gauges raised in my eyes and when the pressures of having low self-esteem, feeling lonely, being bullied into silence, and having a loss of hope for the future reached its allowable pressure level, I exploded uncontrollably.

Each time, I emotionally scarred the women I did not know how to love, when all they wanted was for me to love them like their daddy never did. But I did not know how. I was not their daddy.

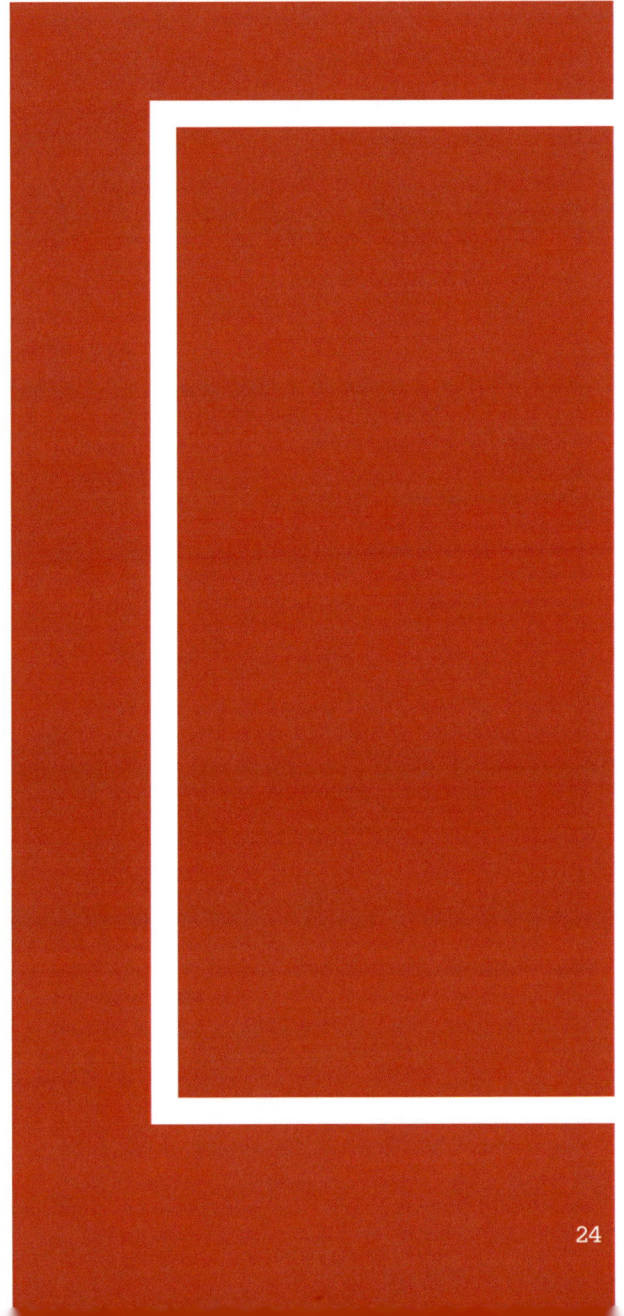

Come On In ;

I'll Show You Why I Did Not Know How To Love Them.

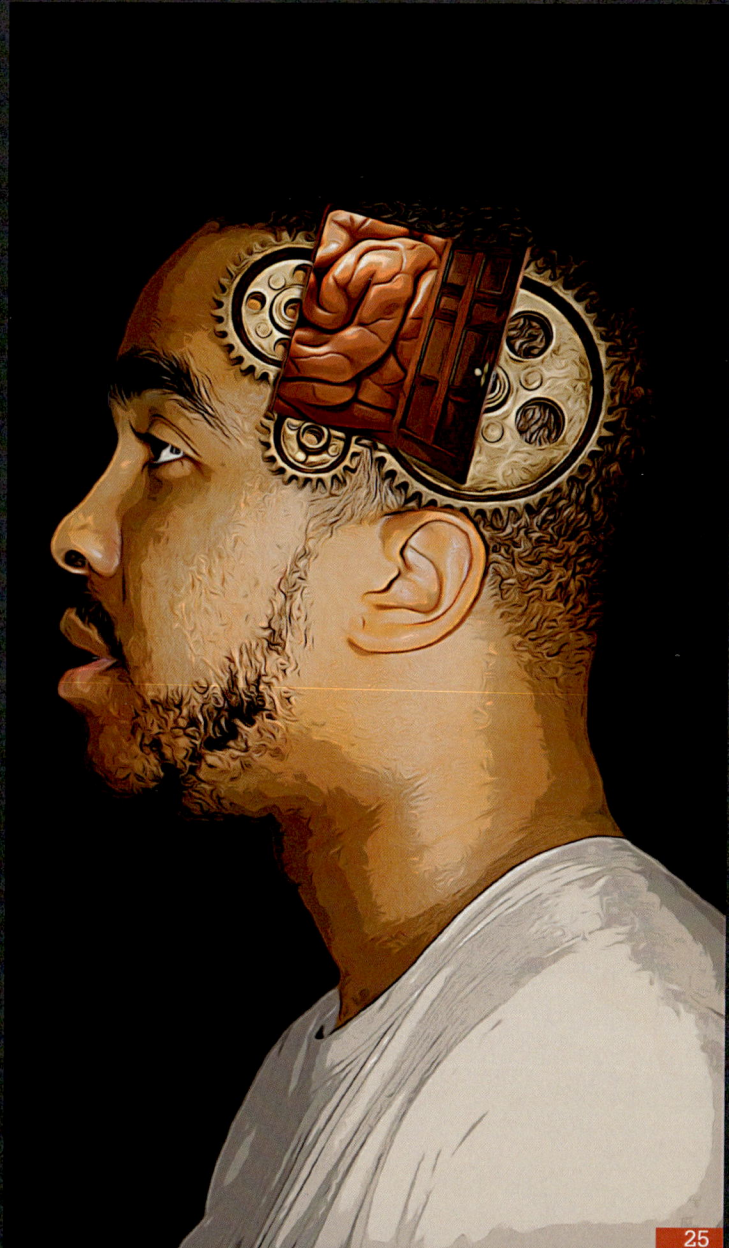

I wish I never had to go to the babysitter's house.

I wish I never had to stay there while my 19-year-old mother went away to work or school.

I wish my babysitter's granddaughter did not have to be there.

I wish she never had me touching on her pussy the way she had me touching on it whenever her grandmother was not there.

"Cookie Crisp cereal for breakfast."

I really wish she had never introduced me to Cookie Crisp cereal.

I wish I had never grown to love them.

Each time I look at the cereal box, I trigger those memories.

I wish I never had to experience being alone with her in her bedroom with the door shut, lights off, and with the television on, because I would have never tried to place my fingers down the pants of a female classmate who was napping during nap time, when I should have been resting too.

She was resting on the cot right next to me at All My Children Daycare.

I was 5

I wish I had never played "Hide Go Get It" with some friends in our low-income housing apartment when my grandparents were not there.

I wish my mother was never sent away to prison.

I wish I was never with one of the girls in the closet making sex sounds, pretending to have sex.

I was 8

Jameel Davis

I wish I had never chosen to play "Hide and Seek" with all the kids in the neighborhood on my grandparents' street.

I wish I had chosen to hide somewhere other than in the neighbor's garage.

I wish it was never dark in there.

I wish one of the teenaged girls who played with us never made me sit on a chair in there, with my pants and underwear down at my ankles.

I wish she did not sit on my lap bottomless, guiding my hands to rub on her breasts and hairy vagina.

I wish the chair had arms to push her away.

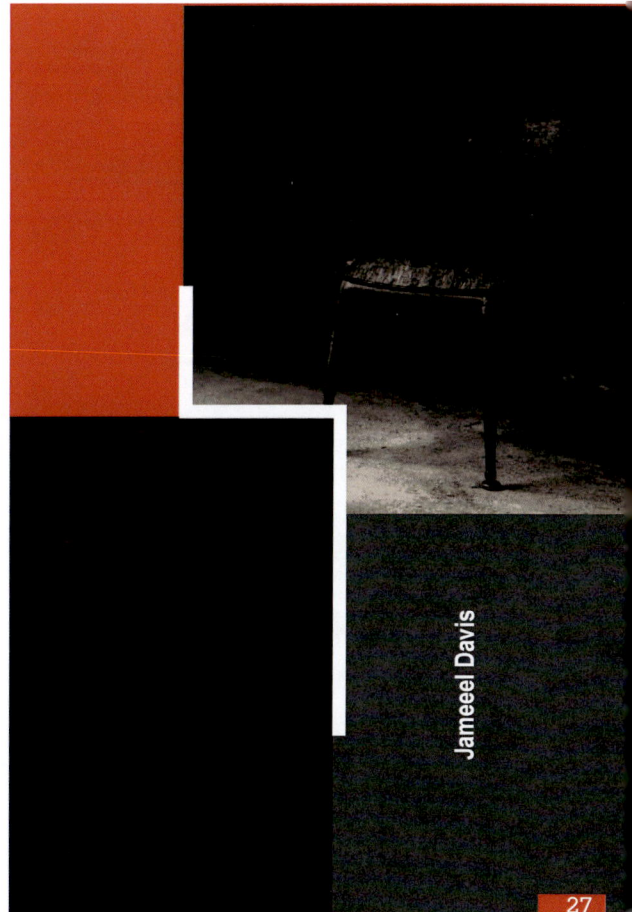

Jameeel Davis

I wish my fingers never touched and smelled like her vagina.

I wish she never put my dick inside her vagina and placed my hands on her ass, while she straddled me like a horse in the chair, while all the other kids laughed and played outside.

I wish she never forced me to be quiet.

I was 9

I wish I was never invited to the birthday sleepover at the neighbor's house who's garage I was molested in.

I wish my grandparents had said no.

I wish the birthday girl's friend, who was also a teenager, did not agree to or have permission from her parents to sleep over.

I wish she had never seduced me to get under her covers and climb up on top of her while everyone else was resting.

I wish she had never unsnapped her bra and guided my head toward her breasts to suck on them.

I wish she had never kissed me in the mouth.

I wish she had never told me not to tell anyone.

I wish I had never listened.

I was still 9

I wish I was not exposed to Blockbuster Movies & MTV Jams that exposed me to, and mimicked sexual content.

I wish I never mimicked their behavior.

I wish I had never learned to dry hump girls.

I wish Feeling on Your Booty by R. Kelly was never one of my favorite R&B Songs.

I wish I never discovered his song at my friend's basement party.

I wish I had never danced to his song with my friend's 13-year-old cousin.

I wish she had never placed my hands on her booty while we danced until the song went off.

I wish the adults were never upstairs drinking and playing cards.

I wish they were down in the basement. I wish they could have stopped her.

I was 10.

I wish my Uncle and his wife had never invited me and welcomed me into their beautiful home.

I wish they never allowed me to sleep in their guest room alone.

I wish my teenage cousin who lived there, but who was not their son, never snuck in my room in the middle of the night

I wish he had left me alone.

I wish he never placed his mouth on my dick and attempted to insert his dick into my ass.

That shit did not feel good. *It did NOT feel good at all.*

I wish I was never introduced to *Fun N Stuff.*

I was 11

I wish I never discovered Masturbation.

I wish my first time ejaculating did not feel like I was peeing on myself.

I wish I never went ram

bling through my grandparents' room while they were away.

I wish I never discovered their Sex Tape collection, which drove me to lose my virginity in the 8th grade to a 7th grade girl who was sexually advanced.

I wish I never mumbled the words suck my dick while we were in lunch period.

I wish she never agreed to do it.

I wish she never walked in the direction of my grandparents' home on her way home from school.

I wish I had never encouraged her to come in knowing that my grandparents were gone.

She gave me the option of a blow job or some pussy.

I wish I had never made any decision.

I wish my first time having sex never felt so good.

I wish I had opened the door when my mother and sister first knocked on the door to my grandparents' home.

That would have saved me from following through with it.

I wish I never had to sneak the girl out of the back door.

I wish she was never there at all.

I wish I had never lost my virginity to the girl who had given my friends and older guys in my neighborhood oral sex after she had sex with me.

I was 14.

I wish I did not have the urge to keep having sex after her.

I wish I did not almost get

caught in the back of an abandoned house with a girl who I desperately wanted to have sex with.

I wish she did not agree to give me oral sex when she denied me vaginal sex.

I wish we didn't have to lie to her mother about looking at newborn kittens when her mother came looking for her when the streetlights came on.

I wish she had never told her role model (who happened to be a stripper) what she did, that I was cute, and that I had a big dick.

I wish they had never stroked my ego.

I was still 14.

I wish I never cried when my girlfriend at the time, who was slightly older than me, who I never had sex with, left me for my uncle because he offered to eat her vagina.

I had never done it.

I was still 14.

I wish I had a father to teach me self-control, self-discipline, emotional intelligence, and how to cherish girls before I lost my virginity.

I wish I had never learned to think with my dick, *but was instead taught to think with my brain.*

I wish I was never thirsty to have sex after losing my virginity.

I wish I was never desperate to have sex with another neighborhood girl, who happened to be unruly and who I knew for sure had sex with many men both young and older.

I wish I was never blinded by her cute face, freckles, and plumped booty.

I wish my family had never taken her in.

I wish I had listened to my friends when they told me not to have sex with her.

I wish I was never so damn hard-headed.

I wish I never had the urge to continue having sex with her, after I had used my whole collection of condoms on her in two days.

I wish I had listened to my Sex-Ed instructor and continued protecting myself.

I wish my dick never hurt, whenever I ejaculated and urinated.

I wish I never messed up my favorite underwear with ugly discharge.

I wish I was never scared to tell my mother.

I wish I never prolonged my visit to the clinic.

I wish I could have saved myself the embarrassment of telling the medical staff about my reason for the visit.

I wish I never had to get that long Q-Tip inserted in my pee hole.

That shit did not feel good. It did NOT feel good at all.

I wish I had never contracted Chlamydia. I am happy that I was cured of it.

I wish I had the courage to give the medical staff her name and contact information.

I wish I was not afraid of public humiliation, embarrassment, and retaliation, because I could have put a stop to her epidemic or at least tried.

I was 15.

I wish I never knew sex felt

much better without a condom.

I wish those affected with STDs, HIV, and AIDS had precaution signs.

I wish I learned how to separate the emotions of sex from love, because I would have not committed myself to the premature, lustful relationships and sexual encounters I had in my adolescence and young adult life.

I wish I learned about parenting way before I had my son.

I wish I was never blinded by his mother's physical appearance.

I wish I never developed the thought that her being with me would rid her of all her problems, and that she would find true happiness with me, and I was still incomplete.

I wish her sex never felt so good. I wish I had never mistaken lust for love.

I wish I had never gotten her pregnant after two months of dating.

I wish she had continued to take her birth control; I wish I kept using condoms.

I wish I was still a Virgin, but still able to have my son.

I wish I had never encouraged his mother to abort his sibling shortly after he was born when I knew she wanted to keep her baby.

I wish I had never added to her pain.

I wish I did not have the fear of being a failing father.

I wish I was successful then.

I wish I was financially stable then.

I was 22

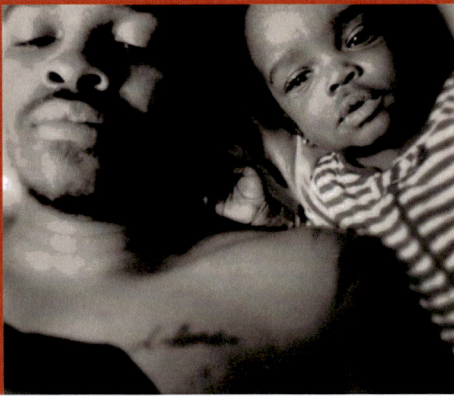

I wish I never mastered the art of sexually satisfying a woman.

I wish the women I had sex with had learned how to separate their emotions of love from sex.

I wish they knew that sex is a part of life and that sex and the pleasing of woman is the nature of man.

I wish they learned to cater to my nature.

I wish my sex was never an intoxicant to the broken women I laid on top of.

I wish I was never their drug.

I wish their sex was never my intoxicant.

I wish I was never addicted to their sex.

I wish they had never grown to become more jealous, more envious, and angrier because of it.

I wish they loved me as much as they did without the sex, as they did when they had it.

I wish I never had the urge to have sex with them.

I wish they had never given me some of the best sex I have ever had.

I wish I had learned to work toward repairing them to their original state of being, before giving them a dose.

I wish they had made me wait until I was a real man before they gave me a dose.

I wish alcohol did not make sex more exciting.

I wish alcohol had given me self-control instead.

I wish something that felt so good did not come with so many unexpected surprises like abuse, neglect, disease, the ruining of families and friendships, mental illness, suicide, and so forth.

I wish I was still a Virgin, But still able to have the life I have today.

I wish I had never been affected by so many social behaviors.

I wish I never Had Sex!

I wish I was still a Virgin.

I CHEATED

My childhood traumas and the lack of a father's love and guidance led me to follow and hand over the power of my mind to the popular crowd, in which I did things that seemed to show no respect for the women I was involved with. Things I thought were cool because it was popular on television shows, movies, in music, and in my environment. Things like thinking with my dick, because the power of my mind did not belong to me during my relationships—you will soon know why it didn't. I had sex with other girls while in a relationship with every girl I was in a relationship with. Yes, I CHEATED...on all of them.

JP Films

I am no longer ashamed of saying I cheated, and I no longer feel the need to lie to the women I cheated on or make up excuses for why I cheated on them. I Cheated, and I did because of various reasons.

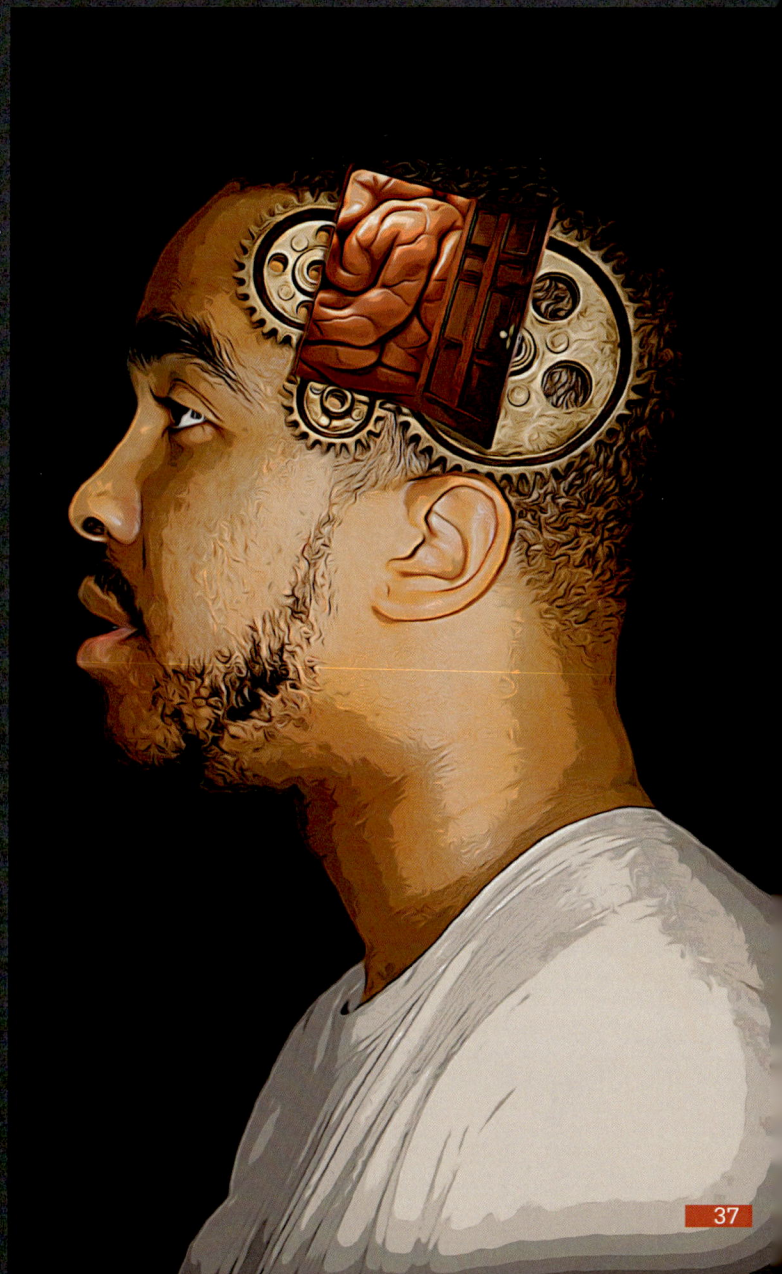

Come On In ;

Let's Find Out Why I Cheated On Them.

WHY DID I CHEAT ON THE WOMEN I WAS IN PREMATURE RELATIONSHIPS WITH?

JP Films

JP Films

I have already given my first reason for cheating: it was the popular thing to do. Growing up, famous male Hip Hop and R&B artists promoted cheating behavior in their lyrics. Being brought up in urban communities plagued by high violence, poverty, and negativity, Hip Hop & R&B music was all I knew. The music went hand in hand with the conditions and behaviors of the people who lived in those environments. Music that kept the cycle of poverty going. Being a young boy forced to live in those environments, singing along to songs of men who promoted cheating—which were played on mainstream radio stations, stereo systems, and in music videos streamed on my television set, computer, and other electronic devices—subconsciously gave me the desire to cheat when I became of age to start having sex.

My subconscious mind, which I had no control of at the time, had been open to the negative influences of those male Hip Hop and R&B artists without me knowing it. Because their music and videos were heavily streamed on radio stations, television, and other electronic devices by everyone in my environment, and because everyone in my environment was copying their behavior, I wanted to do what I heard and saw them do. That was all I was exposed to. I cheated because everyone was cheating. That's how subconscious marketing works; the more you hear it, the more you see it, the more you want it for yourself. It works on those who are mentally weak, and those who do not have control over their mind and behaviors.

I wore some of the clothing, shoes, and jewelry those artists wore just to attract the kind of attention from girls they had attracted to them, so I could have fun **In Between The Sheets** too. Male music artists rapped, sung songs, and made videos that spoke about them having numerous women, and taking and having sex with another man's woman. Even if she was married. These male artists degraded other men—who weren't famous and wealthy—for being poor and not being able to shower their woman with luxury, just to use their fame, money, expensive cars, and jewelry as power to attract the women they were with...with no intention of respecting or keeping her. Just to **hit it and quit it** (have sex with her), making the guy she was with feel worse: less and less of a man.

Women and girls were attracted to that kind of artist, and had more respect for them than the guys who were not rich and famous but who respected and were trying to provide for them the best way they knew how. Women and girls were attracted to these artists because these guys own the radio, television, and the internet, the main media platforms billions of people turn to for entertainment and guidance. The more they heard them and the more they saw them, the more they wanted them for themselves, even if artists referred to them as bitches and hoes in their music.

I cheated on the girls I was in relationships with because the music I was forced to listen to had taken control over and poisoned my subconscious mind, as well as the people in my environment who emulated the behavior of the music I was listening to. I also cheated on them because many of those girls degraded me like their favorite male Hip Hop & R&B artists degraded the guys who were less fortunate than them. Cheating was a disease I had been infected with.

During my childhood and adolescent years, no one ever changed the radio station or the television screen to something more dignifying. I was never told, "Hey Jameel, you should not be watching or listening to that," and I was never encouraged to feed my mind with something more positive, that promoted monogamy, respecting women, and respecting the relationships and marriages of other men. All I knew was to emulate the destructive lyrics from famous male and female Hip Hop & R&B artists.

Growing up, having a main girlfriend and a few secret girlfriends on the side was the guy code; it was the talk of the school, the basketball team, and the locker room. It was all I knew. If a guy could get all his girlfriends on board or in the same bed together, he was labeled The Man. He was praised. I wanted that medal because it was the hot thing to do. I never reached that milestone and when ever I tried, it got too messy with all of the arguments and fights, and I had to throw in the towel. Mainly because I did not have the power to pull it off or the funds to take care of them. I was not balling like their favorite male music artists or backed by mainstream media.

I recall officials at the schools I attended putting together school dances, talent shows, homecomings, and proms that incorporated Hip Hop and R&B music that promoted cheating. The music that was played at these school events were considered clean music by school officials because they were free of profanity. However, the music was never clean even with profanity removed, because the messaging made it dirty. My school teachers and administrators who were not of color had knowingly and unknowingly promoted cheating and the degradation of people of color by the way of the disc jockey's (DJ's) they hired, and the songs they played. The music we danced to was not the same type of music kids at predominantly white schools danced to at their school events, which is one of the many reasons why more white kids grow up and get married than kids of color.

Popular guys at the schools I attended—football and basketball players, music artists, drug dealers, and I—attracted a lot of girls with our talents, image, physical appearance, clothing, shoes, jewelry, money, and other items that were similar to or the same as professional athletes, famous male Hip Hop and R&B artists, and known drug dealers. We received the same attention they received from girls who were attracted to them because we matched their profiles. Girls who were attracted to us subconsciously knew that their chances of getting their hands on celebrities and well-known drug dealers were slim, so they gave their attention to us.

Many girls went to the extent of fighting each other for my attention—even if I was not interested or involved with them—and it was because I was well known, highly intelligent, and I was an athlete. Girls did not want the kind of guys their favorite male artists degraded in their music: those who did not dress nice, were not talented, and who were unable to shower their girlfriends with luxury gifts. They would be publicly shamed by their friends if they found out they gave such guys their attention. "Girl, why do you like him? He broke as fuck. You should talk to such-and-such because he's cute and he got money." Beneath my appearance that matched the profile of someone worthy, I was the guy who was being degraded in popular music songs and in school. I was not famous and I did not have money to buy my girlfriends purses, shoes, or to take them on vacations. Because I did not have the money, this allowed guys who were flashy with their money to attract sex from the girls I was involved with; many gave them sex just to be in their presence, or to say they had sex with a guy with money. Not even to get some of the money the guys were flashing.

Most guys find it amusing when they have women fighting for their attention and love. It strokes their ego. As for me, I never enjoyed when the girls I had sex with—and those I did not have sex with–fought for me.

Many of the girls I was involved with sexually, did not care about which girl's toes they stepped on until they experienced firsthand what it felt like to have their toes stepped on. They did not care who I was involved with. They did not care if it ruined the happiness of the girl I was with at the time. They wanted me to be their intoxicant; they wanted me for themselves. Whenever the girl I was involved with found out about the other girls I was involved with on the side, they called it quits. The girls who were on the side and those who were waiting for their opportunity from afar, were happy that she was gone, and they had more access to me, or a better chance of having me to themselves. Even if it just granted them the opportunity for me to lay on top of them, **Completely Naked.** Those girls felt like they had achieved something amazing because they had taken and had sex with another girl's man. I was still a boy then, but I was a man in their eyes.

It was after I had casual sex with them, that my behavior on and off the court became monitored by them. They wanted to ensure their spot had been secured after glorifying the unhappiness of the girl whose spot they had temporarily taken. Other girls came along soon after and crushed their phalanges as well. Neither of them knew that some of their favorite female artists and groups like TLC and XScape had encouraged the girls they were fighting and competing for my attention and love with, to creep with me in the first place. Songs like "Creep" and "My Little Secret, created their own hairline fractures.

All of the girls I was involved with were dancing to their own degradation as well, but in the same breath wanted me to respect and love them fully. They had very high expectations for the love and re-spect I needed to provide them but did not have high expectations for the people who created the destructive music and images they mim-icked and shook their asses to. I was belittled, degraded, and mental-ly harmed for cheating, but they said nothing about the art ists who planted the disease of cheating in my mind when I was a- child, and who were always encouraging them to cheat with guys who were like them. **They were very contradictory.** I was all types of "Bitches," "Hoe Ass Niggas," and so forth—the same names famous male Hip Hop artists referred to guys who were less fortunate than them—but they were still buying albums and shaking their asses to trendy songs that degraded them openly and publicly in night clubs.

I know what you are thinking.
You are thinking, well if I knew about this,
Why did I cheat anyway?
Why didn't I inform them about this
information?

I was not aware of this at the time. You do not know history is happening when you are in the moment of creating history. Besides, if I knew what I know now back then, they would have not created the space for me to give such an explanation. As far as I knew, I was a **"Hoe Ass Nigga"** in their eyes for cheating on them. They were not trying to hear anything I had to say. Their feelings were hurt, they were drinking Hennessy to numb the pain, looking for their next male intoxicant, and waiting for the weekend to come around so they could shake their asses to the next big degrading song; getting ready to repeat the cycle. The cycle of belittling and degrading men who cheat on them—the same men they found in nightclubs and bars, who fit the profile of someone worthy, who were encouraged to sleep with them in their broken state by the new music they drank Hennessy and twerked to.

"We can talk about you, because you were cheating on him with me— the day after Valentine's Day!

Now, Get Naked and tell him—his card, balloons, candy, flowers, and that fancy room was just numbing cream to the pain he has caused you—that you faked every orgasm with him and everyone else you've been with, until you got that pussy wet for me and had your pussy beg me to dive in face first, turn over and backstroke in it.

Now who ain't shit? "

Not only did I cheat because it was the popular thing to do, but I cheated because the women and men in my family had encouraged me to do it as well. It was instilled in me subconsciously as a young boy with them saying things like,

"You are going to have all the girls when you get older!"
"He's going to be a heartbreaker!"
Or
"Hide your daughters, because he's going
to flatter them with his charm!"

Those repeated phrases and the many others used by the women and men in my family over the years were just as bad as the lyrics in the music of male Hip Hop and R&B artists who promoted cheating. Their repeated phrases, plus the questioning of how many girlfriends I have in and out of school, programmed me to develop the cheating mindset and behavior. When I got to the age where I was allowed to date, and when I got caught cheating, I remember being comforted by my wrongs, by the same people who told me I would be a heartbreaker when I got older. I recall the voices of the men: **"Fuck that bitch! You got all the hoes!"** and the women: **"There are plenty more fish in the sea."**

My mother used to be a firecracker when I was growing up. Whenever I did something wrong, or someone made her upset, she saw red in her eyes and became a raging bull. When I saw the fire in her eyes, that meant she was out to kill. I remember she tore my ass up (whooped me). After getting in trouble, which was never that often, I remember running to my grandmother for soothing and comfort.

Being in her presence felt like nothing ever happened. Her nurturing and love took my mind away from the pain my mother had caused me. **She was my intoxicant.** There was nothing like my grandmother's love.

As I grew older, I tried to take the few relationships I had a little more seriously than the ones I had in my adolescent years. But in each relationship I fell short, because I did not know what I was looking for. I could not identify what genuine love looked like and what-it felt like from a young woman, and I realized I could not because I never received it or was taught what genuine love looked and felt like from my young mother and absent father. I am not saying that my mother did not love me, because she did, and she loved me in her own way. She made sure I was fed, well groomed, I was healthy, had a shelter over my head, and went to school. This is what the government requires parents to do until their children turn sixteen, the legal age where they are able to emancipate themselves, or when they turn eighteen, when they are legally an adult. I am saying she did not teach me how to recognize and receive genuine love from another woman,which caused me to have shortcomings in my relationships. I recall all the fun times well spent with my mother, but I cannot remember the times she would kiss, hold, and comfort me, or show me how a woman is supposed to love me. However, I do remember many of the times she popped off like firecrackers on the fourth of July.

Because I was not able to identify with the love of my mother, and did not receive the love, affection, attention, and emotional guidance I needed from her, I took the risk of searching for love in all the wrong places—with women who I thought would give me the love my mother had never given me. It was very difficult for me to identify with the love of another woman because of that. Women became my intoxicant against the emotional pain I had bottled up and carried over the years. When the women I was in a relationship with became angry with me, they reminded me of my mother; they belittled me, degraded me, and became physical with me like my mother had. When they did that, I ran to women who reminded me of my grandmother, whose comfort took me away from the pain I was enduring...which eventually lead to sex (me Cheating), even if they were already involved with someone else. I needed to get away from the mental and emotional abuse they had caused me... until I was numb enough to return back to them, which eventually did not work out well because I did a poor job hiding my sexual encounters. With each relationship I had, the cycle of behavior repeated.

I could not blame my mother for not showing me how to recognize and receive love from another woman, and I could not blame her for not giving me the love I required at the time because she did not know. She was never taught by my grandparents and my great-grandparents never taught my grandparents, and so forth.

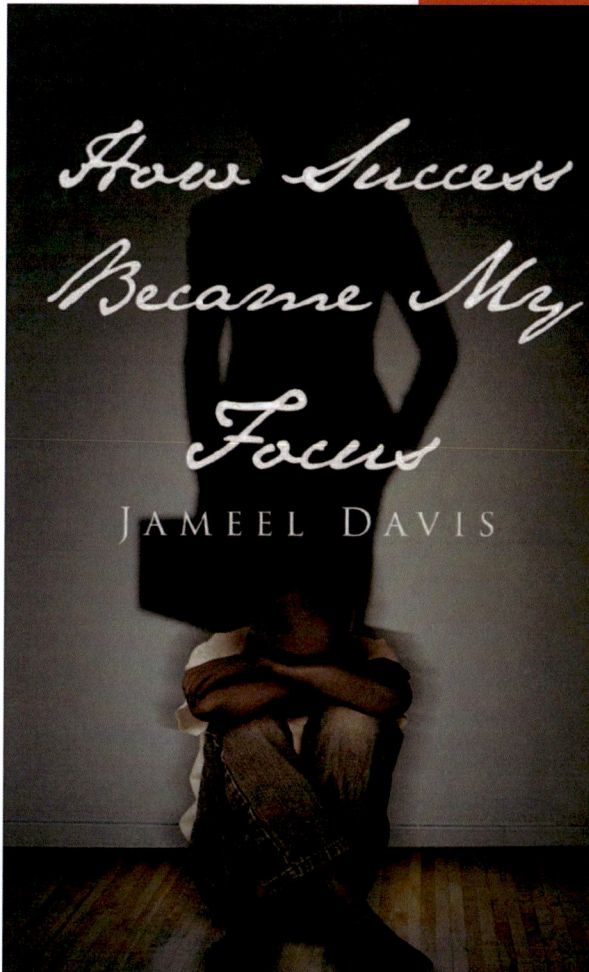

If you read my first book, "How Success Became My Focus," you would know that my mother gave birth to me at a very young age (13) and my grandmother gave birth to my aunt four months after my mother delivered me.

Could you imagine being a pregnant teen without even having sex? Could you imagine being a pregnant teen with the father of your child nowhere to be found? Could you imagine being a pregnant teen mother who was sexually assaulted by her own father when she was just sev en years old? Could you imagine

49

being a young, virgin, pregnant mother without her father, who was serving 20 years in prison for his actions against her and six more for other crimes he had committed? Could you imagine being a young girl and pregnant at the same time as your mother, while still trying to heal from early childhood traumas? Could you imagine being a mother and you are still a kid in the 7th or 8th grade? Could you imagine being a young mom while still developing as a girl? Could you imagine being a young mom and losing your life to the state penitentiary for defending yourself against a girl who harmed you with a weapon, in a state that had no self-defense law?

There is no way I could blame her for not giving me the love I needed and for not showing me how to identify the love I needed from another woman. For all I know, **SHE DID HER FUCKING BEST** and her best helped shaped me into the man I am today. My mother was battling her own traumas, which got in the way of her loving me properly, and because of that, my traumas got in the way of developing a successful relationship with the women I was involved with.

Jedi Art

Both my mother and grandmother have grown to provide me with the love I needed over the years, and this love has taught me how to identify what love looks and feels like from another woman.

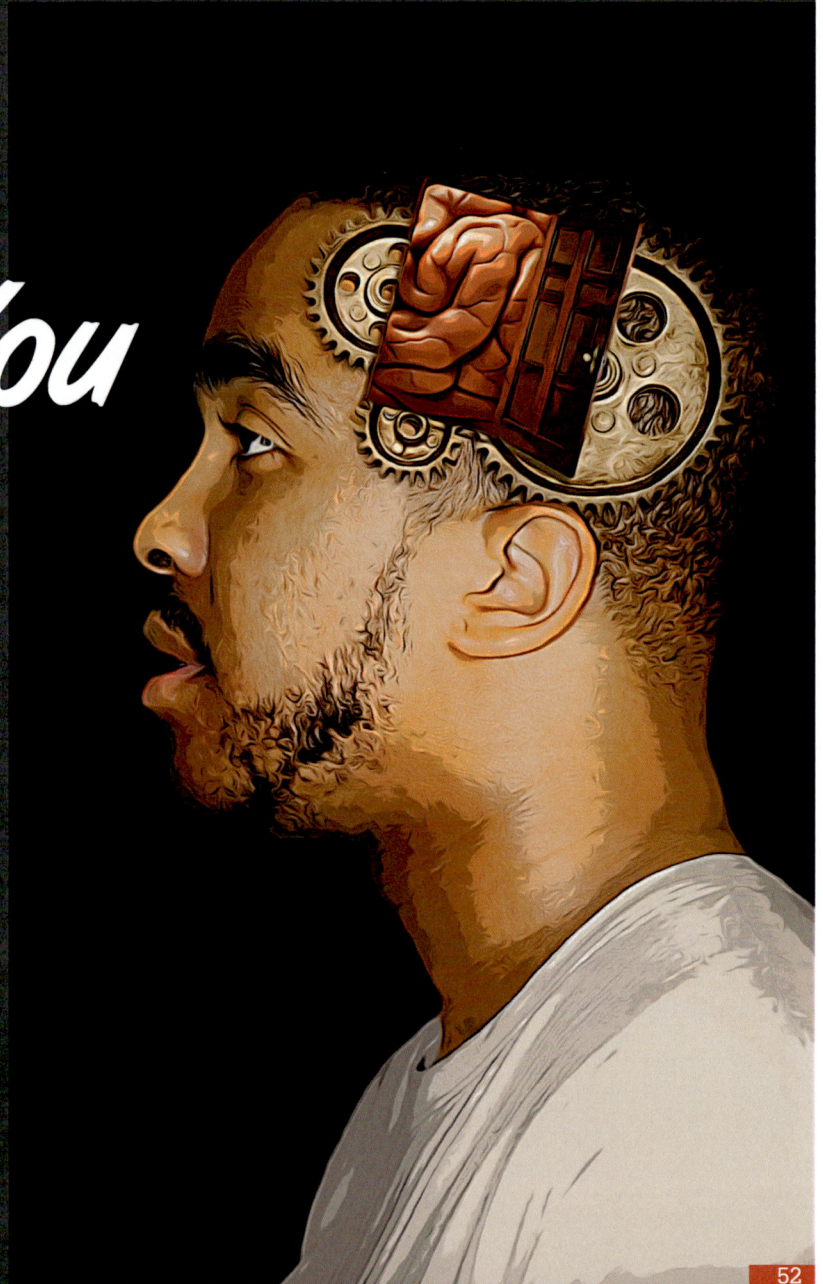

Come On In ;

I'll

Show You

How

"The best way to my heart is through my mother & grand-mother. If you have not taken the time to schedule a sit down with either of them to gather my favorite foods, their recipes to make them, and the GPS coordinates to my control center, your chances at success with me may be slim."

As I mentioned before, my mother and grandmother have grown to provide me with the love I require and have taught me how to identify what love looks and feels like from a woman. They taught me that *if a woman cannot treat me as good as they treat me, then that woman is not worthy of me.* My mother has not physically disciplined me since I was in elementary school and I do not think my grandmother ever has. They have only lifted their hands to hug, hold, and help me during times of need and to show their appreciation for the man I have become. In my presence, they have not fixed their lips to yell at me out of anger or slander my name, but only to build me up and cheer me on from the sidelines and in the stands.

Both my mother and grandmother have encouraged me to get to the point where I am now in life, where people must *come to me with respect or don't allow them to come to me at all,* because I should not accept nor tolerate the uncontrolled emotions and behaviors of others. Once I reached this point and developed the ability to ignore the negative influences of others, *I was able to see and move forward toward a brighter path ahead. I also learned that another woman's mommy and daddy issues are not my problem,* they are *hers.* If she wants my guidance in healing I may assist, but she must take the initiative herself to heal her wounds and meet me where I stand as a mature, self-disciplined, educated, respectful, and responsible adult, before presenting herself to me for a relationship. *Hurt people, hurt people.* If I allow a woman to come into my life and she cannot meet me where I stand, she will soon impose her problems and pain on me for me to fix, which I cannot do. This will weigh down my crown that she cannot help me pick up. If I allow this kind of woman to stay in my life, she will soon grow to hate me for my failed attempts at helping her with her problems and instead blame me for all the problems and pain her parents, previous boyfriends, or husbands caused her.

"If she cannot treat you nearly as good as we treat you or as good as you treat yourself, then she isn't worthy of you. Whenever a woman fixes her mouth to speak unkindly to and of you, it's time to go!"

Healthy relationships were never the topic of discussion during my childhood and adolescent years, so a lot of social influences played a big part in me cheating on the women I was in premature relationships with. I had no positive role models to tell me how the poisoned music and images destroyed colored families and how it was preparing me for a life of failed relationships. It was never advertised on television, radio, or shown to me in my environment how a woman was supposed to be loved and respected, or how to build a healthy family. It was not mandatory for me to learn how. As I mentioned before, my mind was controlled by the negative thoughts and behaviors of the "popular" crowd.

It felt as though the people who took on the educator roles in the communities where I lived wanted me to excel academically, but not psychologically, to help reverse the conditions of the people in my community. They wanted me to be book smart, but to still dance in my own degradation to the beat of the drums of Hip Hop and R&B artists who did not promote healthy black relationships.

There was no blueprint that taught me how to transition from adolescence to adulthood. I never learned how to date properly. All I knew was to follow the behaviors of the popular crowd and the voices of tradition. Although I have cheated on the women I was in premature relationships with, I never did it to intentionally cause them harm. Since learning and understanding my reasons for cheating and owning up to my actions, I have grown to operate from a place of oneness, where I add the highest value I possibly can to every woman and person I come in contact with, continuously and unconditionally. I treat every woman fairly and with respect because my seeds of generosity, empathy, and kindness grow to become healing plants. I am now deliberately healing those who may be battling the disease of cheating—the disease I once had to battle alone—which will allow them to recognize genuine love from another man and avoid men who do not have their safety and best interest at heart.

I forgive my mother for not knowing how to provide me with the love I needed at the time, and my elders and ancestors for not knowing how to love and teach love. I forgive my father for his absence, and I forgive my abusers for the pain they caused me—because I understand the source. I apologize again to every woman and person I have ever harmed physically, mentally, and emotionally, as a result of the pain I endured. And I apologize for unintentionally giving my mind to the negative influences of others in my environment, in music, in movies, and on television.

YES, I CHEATED!
BUT I AM TRULY SORRY!

JP Films

"FINDING THE LOVE OF A BLACK MAN"

Remove the penis and you lose the woman.

Rather you deposit it in the womb of another woman, it malfunctions, it gets amputated, or you just are no longer sexually interested in her. Remove the penis and she will remove herself and all things attached to her.

Sex is biological and love is spiritual; without sex, she loses the emotional attachment and the need to stick around — sex which she associates with love.

Remove the penis and you lose the woman, unless she knows the difference between sex and love.

"A Good Man who is Wrongfully Convicted will Lose his Woman to a Bum with a Working Penis and a Brother in the Military will Lose his Wife to His Brother or Best Friend with an Available Penis who Exhausted his Savings Account."

(More on Page 157)

#CompletelyNaked

No Man Wishes To Be Challenged About Everything He Think, Say And Do By His Woman.

If You Don't Trust Him or Feel Secure with Him, Let Him Go.

Set Him Free; for He is Better Off without your Limitations on His Potential and with such freedom he can get the best out of himself.

In the summer of the year 2015, at the age of twenty-five, I reached out and tried to work things out with the mother of my son (Jah) again. It had almost been two years since we broke up, shortly after I graduated from Kent State University. I was still a young, black, broke man buried in college debt when I contacted her with the idea. I informed her that I would be moving into a nice home in a suburb of Cleveland, Ohio, and I would love it if we could take another shot at the American Dream of being a family in a beautiful home with a white picket fence.

It was mid-August. After talking things over in detail for the next week or so, and after showing her the pictures of the home, she was excited about the opportunity and moved on in. Just like before, we worked for a little while trying to rekindle what we had in the beginning: a lustful relationship without proper healing, no foundation of friendship, morals, principles, values, or a concrete plan about how to make it work. Just wishful thinking. Like all of my previous relationships, we crumbled like a vegan cake without the egg (which is the primary structure-builder in cakes that are non-vegan). With the egg removed from our relationship, again, we fell flat. With the egg removed from our relationship—proper healing, a solid foundation of friendship, morals, principles, values, and a legit plan to make it work—our spark was short lived. It was blown out and we could not ignite it again. We both grew to be angrier with one another. I cheated on her, for reasons I mentioned in Chapter One, and I got caught.

Early November, the end of our relationship, I began to see how her bottled up anger that she carried over the years from various sources like her parents, relatives, other people, and the added pain I brought on affected her role as a mother to our son who was three years old at the time. He was not receiving the love and attention he required from her: the kind of love and attention that was absent from my mother when I was younger.

I remember him calling for her, "Mommy, Mommy, Mommy," while she was browsing the internet and texting on her cellular phone, and she would ignore him a while before answering "WHAT?" or attending to his needs. She would ignore him, then shout at him, and not shower him with affection because she was angry with me and he is my son. I did not want my son to continue experiencing what I went through growing up with my mother, and I definitely did not want him to observe and be affected by the problems his mother and I were experiencing. So I took action, I swallowed my emotions, and kept my frustrations inside. Instead, I attracted women who could shower him with love and affection: relatives, friends, colleagues, or women I was causally having sex with. I wanted him to be around women who have respect for men of color, so his subconscious mind could program him to identify what love looks and feels like from another woman.

In mid-November, Jah's mother approached me and informed me that she would be moving out of the home in early February 2016. I was excited about the news and it seemed as if February took its precious time to come with all of the tension that was building up. After she informed me of her decision to move, she asked if she could live rent free and contribute a portion of her earnings towards bills and food, so she could save money to move out. I do not know why I said she could stay under those terms; I should have told her to make arrangements because the next couple of months were hell.

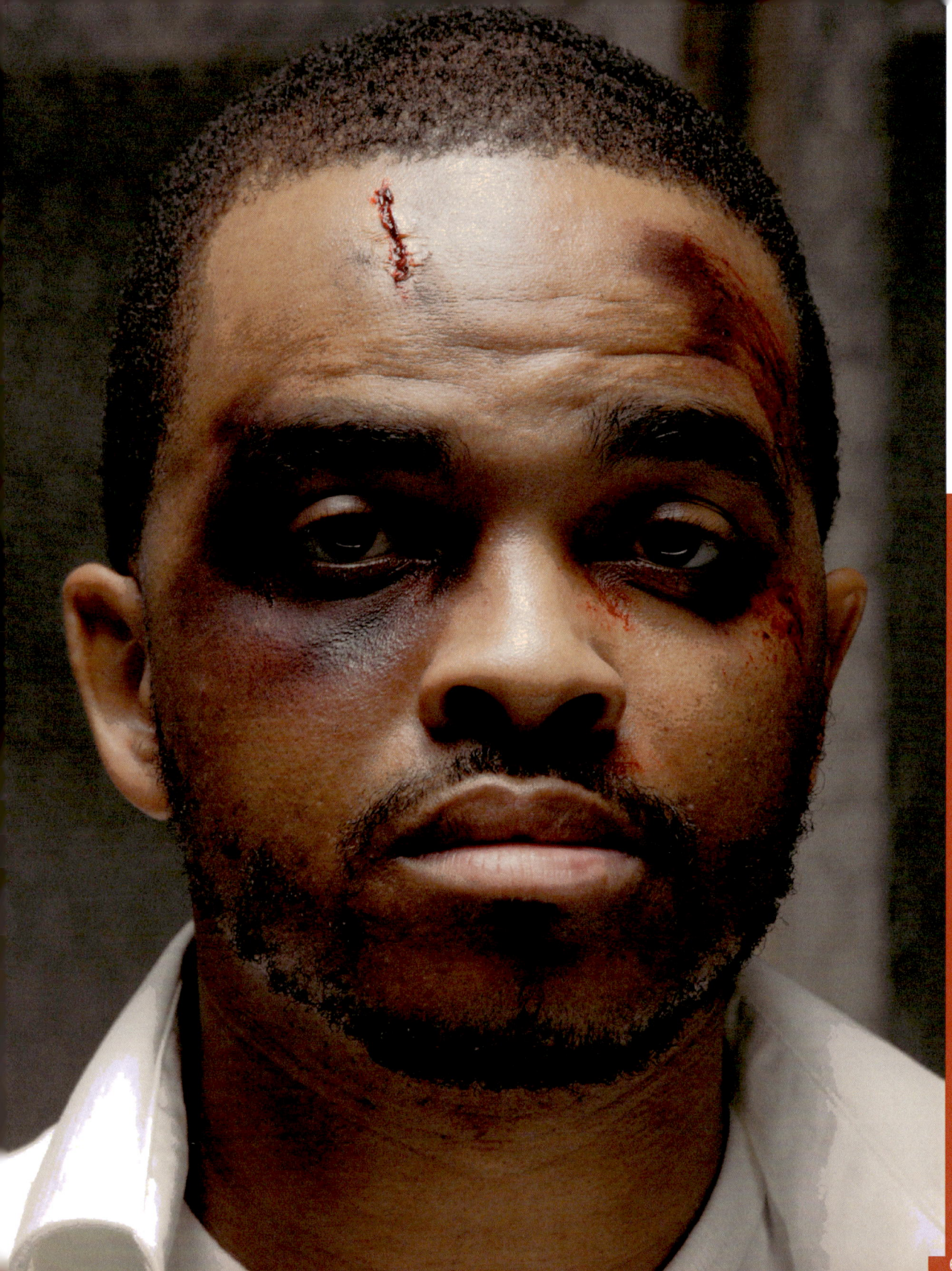

It was very difficult to share my home with someone I was no longer able to engage in sexual activity with, who I was not friends with, who was not providing my son with the attention he desired, and who did not own up to her end of the bargain. She did not contribute to utility bills, housing products, cleaning the house, or meal expenses like she agreed to. Instead, she watched me struggle to do it all on my own as she lounged around, saving her moving money, stuffing her belly with the food I prepared, juicing up my electricity, gas, water, sewage, and internet bills. As if I was her pimp. **Bills are high during the winter months, and I was a broken man trying to climb up the ladder from debt,** while still trying to exemplify good character and leadership for my three-year-old son.

It became increasingly difficult to share my living space with her when I prepared meals for my female friends and invited them over. It was awkward very awkward for everyone. She even gave me problems for doing so. She was already living rent- and bill-free, plus she wanted to have control over me and my house. It wasn't going to happen! In my mind, it was already bad enough I allowed her to take my kindness for weakness. She knew my emotions had been swallowed, and my frustrations were locked away, and believed I would not put her out of the house in front of my son. However, her selfishness and attitude were not going to keep me from entertaining the company of females in my home. I was no longer going to be bullied into silence; I needed that good, positive female energy in my home. The kind my son's mother did not provide.

Author NeeNee Marie

I understand the great deal of pain I caused her by Cheating and not being able to provide her the love she required, but I wondered if her selfishness was her way of making me pay for the pain I caused?

I grew more upset each day she was there, but as I previously did, I kept my anger and frustration bottled up because I did not want to do anything to jeopardize everything I worked hard for. I did not want my son to see me in a way that did not show good character and self-control. So, I transferred my energy into positive things like sports, writing, partying, and creating beautiful memories with my son, my family, and friends. When my son's mother's move out date rolled around, I naturally broke my morning sleep after completing a 12-hour work shift, and noticed she was still in my home. She had still not contributed like she agreed to back in November, and was very disrespectful towards me.

After climbing up out of bed, I heard her voice coming from downstairs in the living room. I followed the sound and made my way down the steps and into the living room where she was sitting on the couch holding a conversation on her cellular phone. I interrupted her conversation, and confronted her about moving out that day. I said to her, "I thought you were moving out today," and she replied, "I forgot to tell you, I gave you the wrong date." She then told me her new moving date which was a week or two out and said she needed to stay longer.

Jameel Davis

I did not give her the same response I gave her when she asked me if she could stay rent-free back in November; I could not take her being in the house with me any longer. My blood reached its boiling point and red filled my eyes. I could not allow her to continue to watch me struggle to tread water, while I was *suffering in silence* because of the pain and demons I was already battling before we first started dating. She had to leave my home at that moment. I told her she had to go.

She hung up her phone after the unexpected news and called me all types of *"Bitches," "Hoe Ass Niggas,"* and so forth in front of our son. The same names famous male Hip Hop artists used to refer to guys who were less fortunate than them in their music who she had been listening to and shaking her ass to in night clubs. The same ones who openly disrespected women and encouraged her to dance in her own degradation.

She called her mother over, they packed her belongings, and she left my home with my son. When she left, I screamed as loud as I possibly could, releasing all of the built-up anger and frustration I had locked inside of me. I felt relieved.

Author NeeNee Marie

Neither of us were ready to be in a relationship; we were damaged long before meeting each other. Through me, she was looking for the love of her absent father, and I could not give her the love she needed. I could not give her the love she required because I was not her father, was never taught how to love a woman, and I was still battling my own traumas and demons on top of the pain she caused me. Also, I could not give her the love she required because she was not happy and secure within herself. Her unhappiness reflected on those around her, including me and our son. There was nothing I could have done to make her feel good about herself and to be happy with me, even if I had not cheated on her.

She was battling her own internal demons at the time we met, which eventually **I had to pay for.** I was looking for her to give me the love my mother never gave me, which she was not able to do because she was not my mother and she was never taught how to love a man. Also, she could not give me the love I required because I was not fully happy and secure within myself. As a result, I received the opposite of love.

The pain she had bottled up over the years from all those who had caused her pain—her parents, and past boyfriends, and whoever else, plus the pain I had caused her—exploded on me and our son in the form of degradation, neglect, and selfishness. We were both an emotional wreck, we were both hurting each other, and there is no telling what would have happened if we stayed together in that house any longer. To me, our breakup was the best decision for the both of us.

After my son's mother and I parted ways, I went through what I called a **Re-Evaluation Period.** It was a period of almost two years, when I gave myself a self-analysis and went on a journey of finding and learning to love myself. I grew tired of creating a vicious cycle of pain, whether I was the perpetrator or the victim. I put a halt to dating and seeking relationships during that time. Before I began my Re-Evaluation Period, I realized I had invested a lot of my time and energy into broken women. That time got us nowhere but to a place where we became angrier with one another, instead of investing my time and energy in healing, finding self-love, and finding the real me. Investing in those women who were broken was hindering my growth. It was time that I had found me: peace of mind, developing pure self-determination, self-discipline, self-worth, love, acceptance, wealth, and friendships.

Before I share the process of my revaluation period with you, I would first like to opely apologize to the mother of my son.

Come On In ;

And See What I Have To Say To Her.

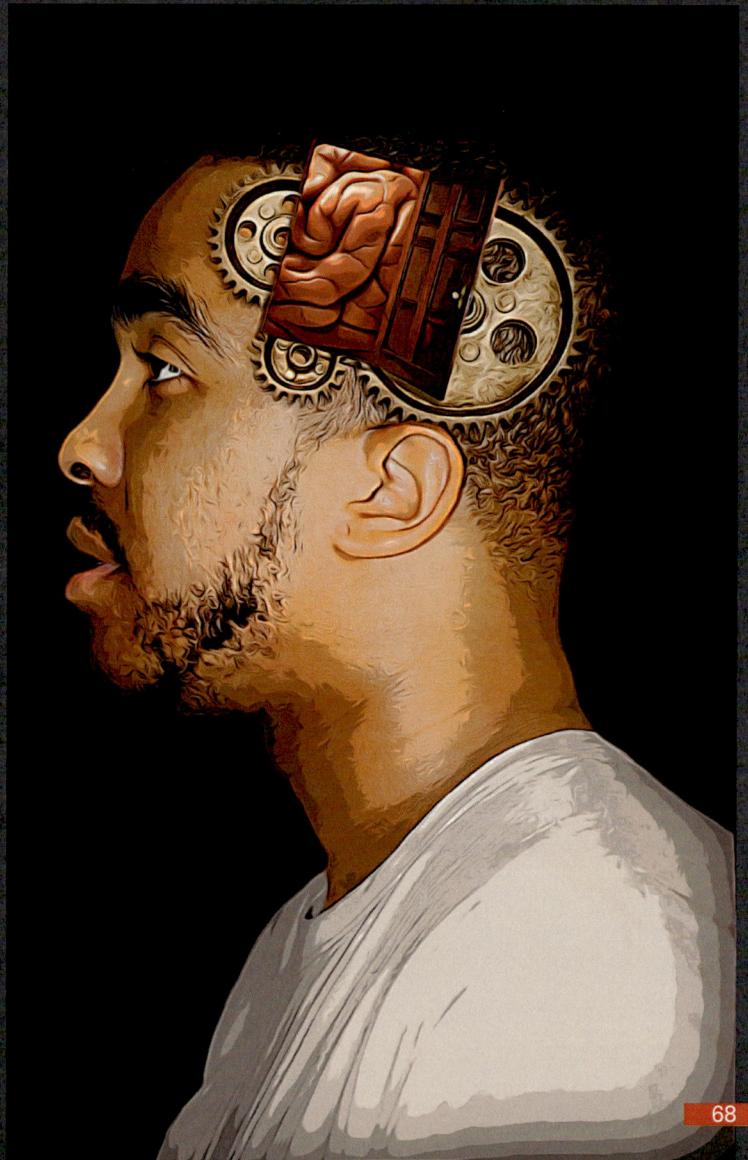

To the Mother of my Son,

As tears begin to fall out of my right and left eyelids, and mucus starts to run out of my nostrils, dripping onto my shirt writing this, I would like to openly apologize for not being the man you imagined me to be when you and I were together. I thought I could be that man for you in my broken state, and I wanted Side A, the picture-perfect relationship advertised in movies, television shows, and on social media profiles for us—but it was all an illusion. I did not know how to make it happen. I figured if I copied the behavior of the men seen on the big screen, our relationship would flow naturally. But I was wrong. I was so hurt and damaged inside that I could not recognize myself in the mirror, but yet I tried to force you to be real with me. I was just living the best way I knew how.

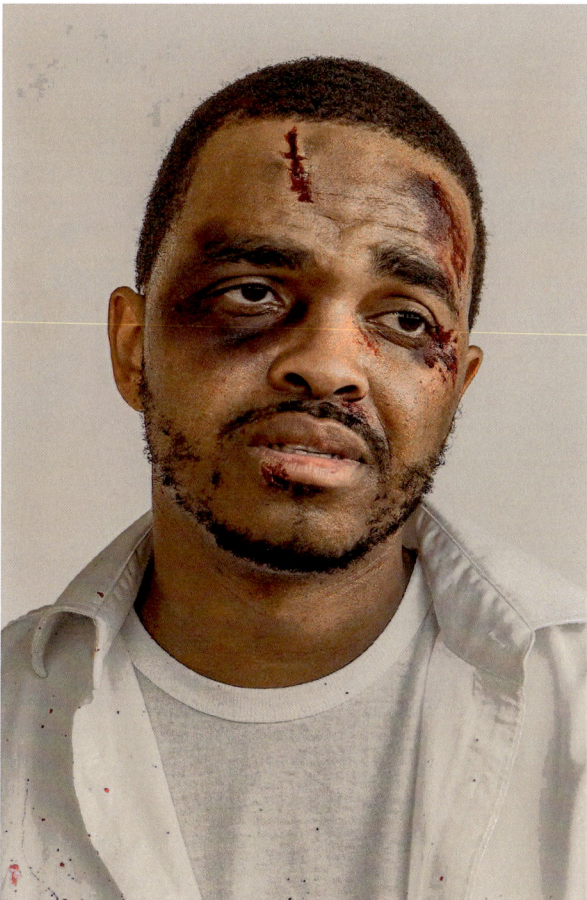

I did not know about Side B—the blood sweat, and tears those in real healthy relationships have invested into for their court to be as beautiful as it is—and the strong foundation of friendship they built prior to forming their relationship. Also, I was unaware of the many months and years of rehearsing actresses and actors spent creating picture-perfect fairytales of happy couples who do not experience problems.

My subconscious mind was open to that. Not knowing how dating and relationships worked for me, not having parents or anyone around me who demonstrated healthy relationships—or who steered me away from the poisonous music, images, and behaviors of the people in my environment—I was not able to be the man you needed me to be. As a result, I caused you more pain. I am not asking you to forgive me or asking for us to get back together; I just wanted to openly apologize for the pain I caused you, and to let you know that I am truly sorry for not having full control of my mind, body, and spirit before my mind was fully developed.

Our experiences and my upbringing have helped me become a better father to our son, and true man and leader for men and women across the world. I hope my apology and this book, encourage you to heal your wounds—those I and others have inflicted on you—to find self-love, self-happiness, to bring you closer to your purpose, and to help you attract a guy who can provide you with the love you require. And in return: you provide him with the same.

Jameel

Tyrone Willis

Jessica Bacon

During my Re-Evaluation Period, I separated who I wanted to be from who the world wanted me to be. I focused on my deepest thoughts, feelings, and emotions, and why I did the things I did. I dug deep within myself, figured out what I needed and wanted out of life, and made it my duty to secure them. I eliminated many distractions and took many risks that challenged me for the better. I forgave those who brought me pain and just focused mainly on myself, engaging in activities that I enjoyed.

I learned to love myself during my Re-Evaluation Period. Learning to love myself required me to first be true to myself, think for myself, respect myself, heal the wounds—those I and others have caused me—take care of my health, and invest fully into my goals and dreams.

I learned during my self-discovery period that my happiness reflects on everyone around me, and nobody can make me happy. Self-happiness is an internal state that only I can create myself.

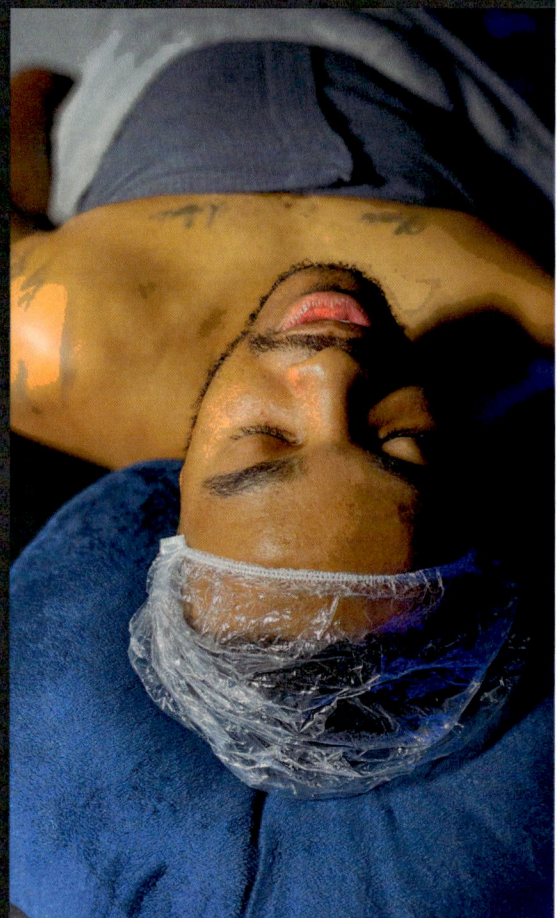

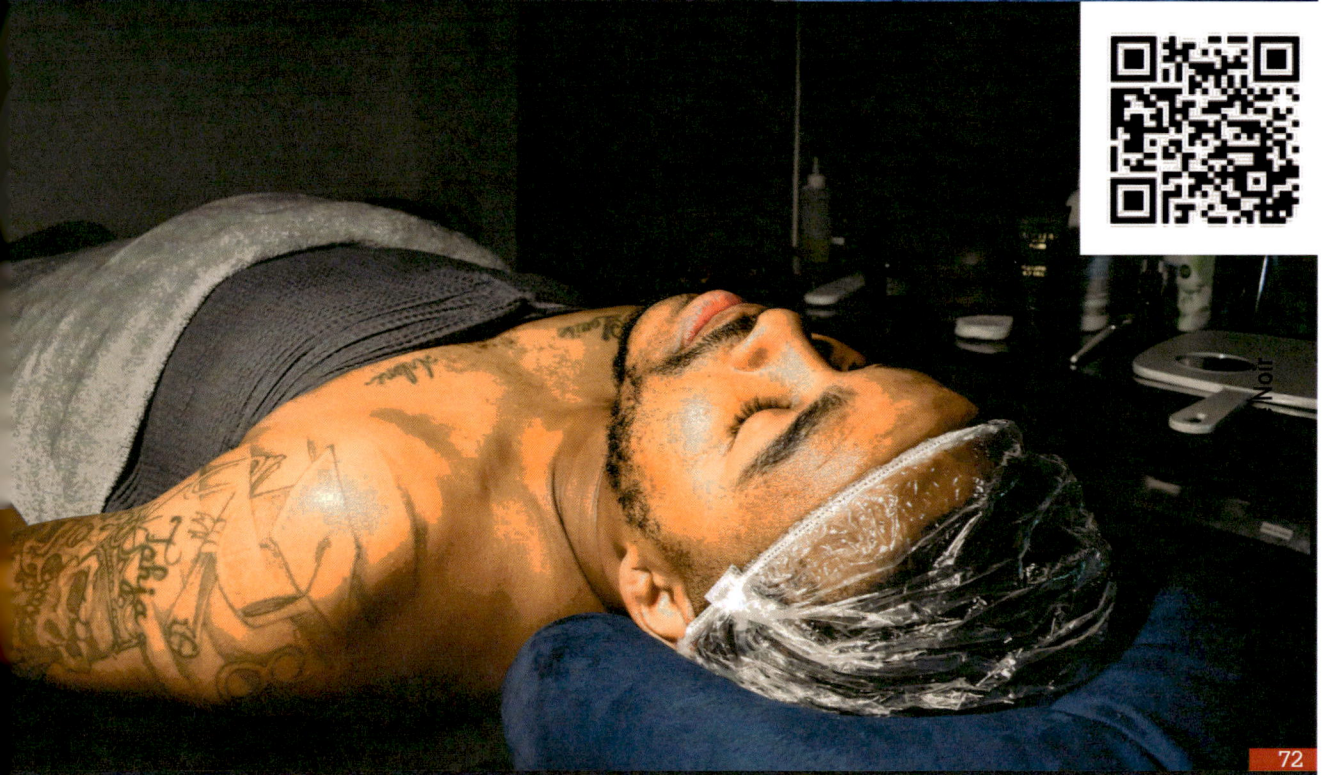

I Love Myself! Therefore, I Must Respect Myself. Because I Love and Respect Myself, I Must Love and Respect Others.

Those who know me know that I love myself because my actions reflect it; because I love myself, there is no doubt that I love and respect others.

Not only did I learn to love myself during my time away from dating and relationships, but I also learned self-control: how to manage my emotions. The things that once triggered me to become angry and frustrated no longer got the best of me. I learned to **limit my reactivity** – when someone says something I do not like, causes, or attempts to cause harm to me, instead of reacting negatively I pause, breathe deeply, and think of a skillful response using non-violence. This exercise allows me to prevent the negative energy of others from affecting me negatively. Sometimes I go as far as ignoring people and or smiling at them, which also blocks their negative energy from affecting me.

Understanding myself, my upbringing, and the pain I have experienced from other women, has allowed me to recognize my values and worth. From afar, I can also recognize women who have bottled up anger and pain inside, which allows me to protect myself from attracting their soul-ties, allowing me to maintain my peace and sanity. ***Hurt people, hurt people.***

After finding self-love and restoring myself back to my ***natural (unbroken) state,*** I was able to learn how to date effectively. I learned how to evaluate women before making them comfortable in my life, and create a solid foundation of friendship before securing an intimate relationship. Although I am healed and able to date effectively, many women who spark interest in me are not healed, are emotionally needy, and do not know how to — nor do they desire to — date effectively, which ruins the opportunity of a great friendship ever happening. Many have looked for me to provide a quick fix to their pain (be their intoxicant), without first figuring out if I'm a good man or not.

They take a look at me, see success, crave me, and do not challenge me at all. Many are carrying childhood traumas and pain from other men and will never be truly happy with themselves or anyone else, because they do not give themselves enough healing time to find a man who is good for them. Because they are emotionally needy, they will accept any man—even if he is not right for them. Like Dr. Umar Johnson said, "They have a magnet inside that says, **I need a man, I have low self-esteem, I need attention."** When damaged women are out searching for a man because they are emotionally needy, their main focus is not the wellbeing of those men, but instead their own pain, their needs and the things those men possess they think will make them happy. They do not focus much on the problems and pain the men they are involved with—or trying to be involved with—are enduring. They are blinded by their money, cars, and clothing.

Many of the women I was involved with and who tried to date me believed all they had to do for me was to look good, cook, clean, and give me sex whenever I asked for it. Many believed that, because that is what they saw the women in their family or friends do, or what they saw actresses on television and movies do for the men they were involved with. They were wrong. I require much more than that. I require the same exact treatment women require: attention, love, kindness, affection, direction, and guidance. More importantly than all of that, I wish to be respected by women, heard by women, cared for by women, and to receive assistance from women during times of need. A woman's physical features, her ability to cook and clean, and her love alone will never be enough for me or any man. Especially if he is broken.

Come On In ;

Allow Me To Show You Why It Won't Be Enough.

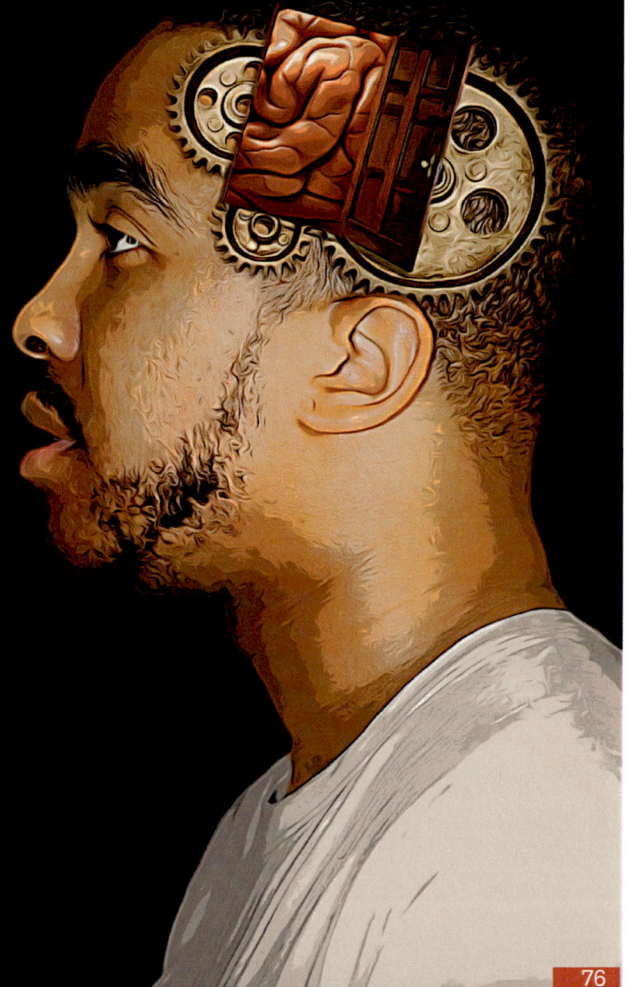

During my previous relationships, which were all short lived, I battled many other demons (other than childhood traumas) that women I was involved with were not able to assist me with. Demons like depression and anxiety that were caused by six basic fears: the fear of poverty, fear of criticism, fear of ill health, fear of loss of love of someone, fear of old age, and the fear of death. Because I was battling those demons and could not turn to any of them to help me overcome a different kind of pain I was experiencing at the time, there were times where I was not interested in being intimate with them. I did not want to have sex; I did not want to be cuddled up. I wanted to be left alone. Because I was intimately, sexually, and emotionally unavailable at times, they formed the following conclusion: "You must be fucking another Bitch!"

Author NeeNee Marie

The main reason I could not turn to them and allow them into my password-protected vault was because society had conditioned me to never show a sign of weakness and emotion, and if I did...I was weak. I was not a man. Also, I could not turn to them and allow them in because they all believed they were only required to give me their good looks, sex, warm meals, and a clean home. They were not aware that catering meant more than what they had offered me. Had they been taught properly by the women in their life, they would have known that nurturing was not only required during motherhood, but for as long as they lived, and to be provided to anyone who is battling any sicknesses and pain. Just as mothers naturally nurture their young when they know something is not going well with their baby, the women I was involved with would have recognized what was bothering me, and nurtured my wounds had they been taught properly. You don't hear women say to their baby: **"You Must Have Been With Another Mother."**

I have to go much deeper regarding the source of my depression and anxiety.

Allow me to invite you into another part of my vault that I had password protected at the time.

Come On In

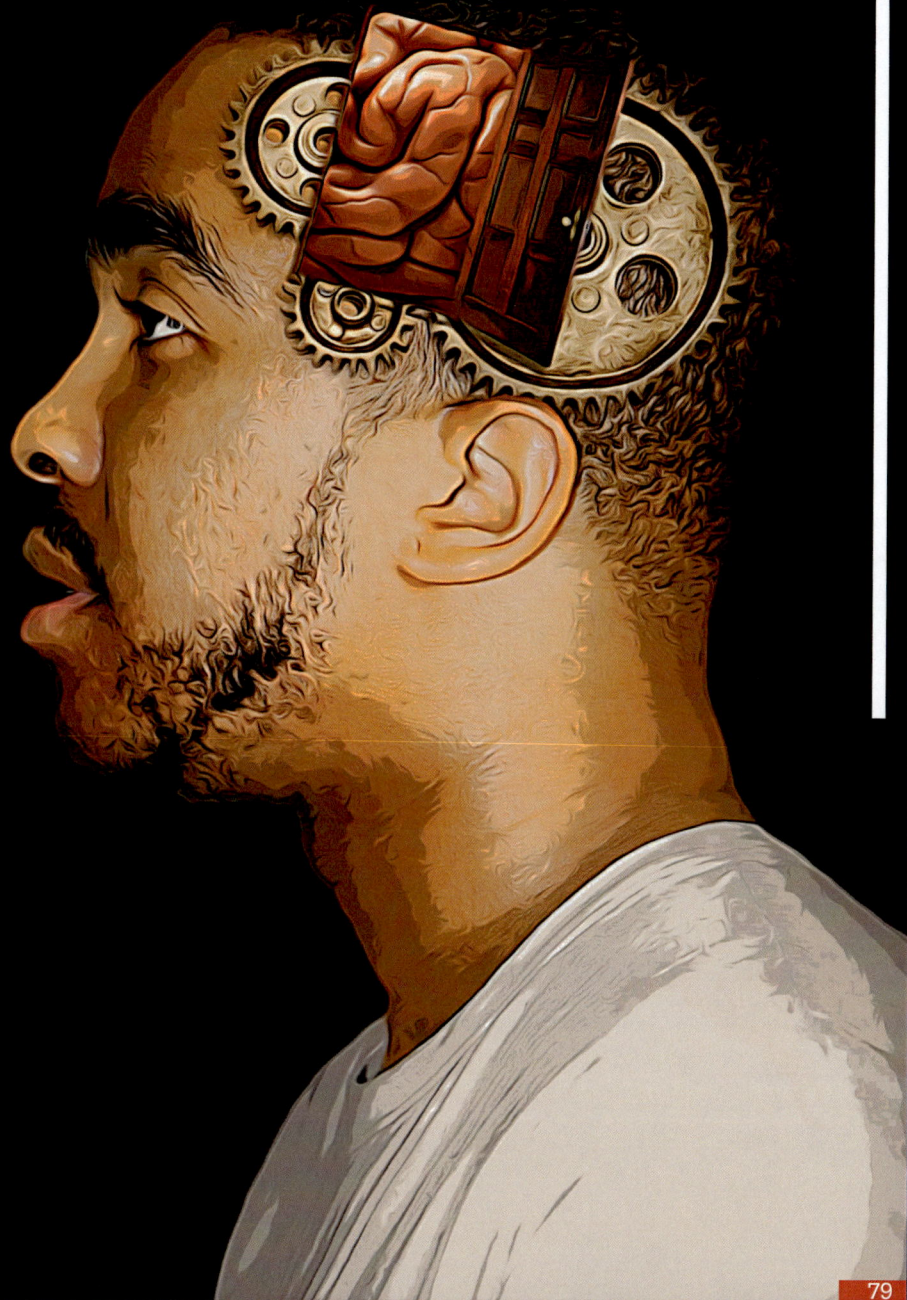

America is a battlefield for People of Color, especially for colored men. The moment my young mother found out she was pregnant, I was already programmed for failure. Mansfield B. Frazier, author of "From Behind The Wall; Commentary on Crime, Punishment, Race and The Underclass By A Prison Inmate" quoted:

"Young mothers are often found delivering low-birth weight babies, which results in him growing up with learning deficiencies. Young boys with learning deficiencies are often found in single mother homes, in poverty dominated neighborhoods. Many single mother homes don't have a foundation of academic and economic education, intimacy, compassion, love, and respect. As a result, young boys fall behind in school, become distant from love and affection from women, and eventually end up on the streets, fostering a life of drugs, alcohol, and criminal activity, in which many end up in the jail and the prison system."

Although I was not born at a low-birth weight and did not have learning deficiencies, I still grew up in a single mother home in poverty dominated environments, without a foundation of academic and economic education, limited to no intimacy, compassion, love, and respect. I fell behind in the first grade because of my attendance, which resulted in me repeating the first grade, being bullied and made fun of by the students who had advanced to the second grade. I also grew distant from love and affection from women because of the broken foundation I had. There are little to no resources in impoverished neighborhoods that are working toward reversing the current conditions, minds, and behaviors of the people who are living in those environments. When boys and men of color are denied the opportunity to learn, earn a living, raise a family, and live rewarding lives like the elite class in America, nobody helps, let alone seem to care enough. Not even our own women, for what it seems like.

3KP Marketing

Our oppression has turned many of our own girls and women against us, and America **designed this way of life for us since arriving here** in 1619. Most of us have become immune to a life of hopelessness, betrayal, and defeat to the point that we are no longer able to **recognize ourselves when we look in the mirror.**

We find difficulty in recognizing people who are here to help us become better men. Those of us who have managed to escape from a life of poverty and incarceration, who have received an education, secured a position with a company, or have opened our own businesses and who are now living a good life, are still in danger of being defeated by systematic oppression.

Come On In ;
Allow Me To
Show You
Why.

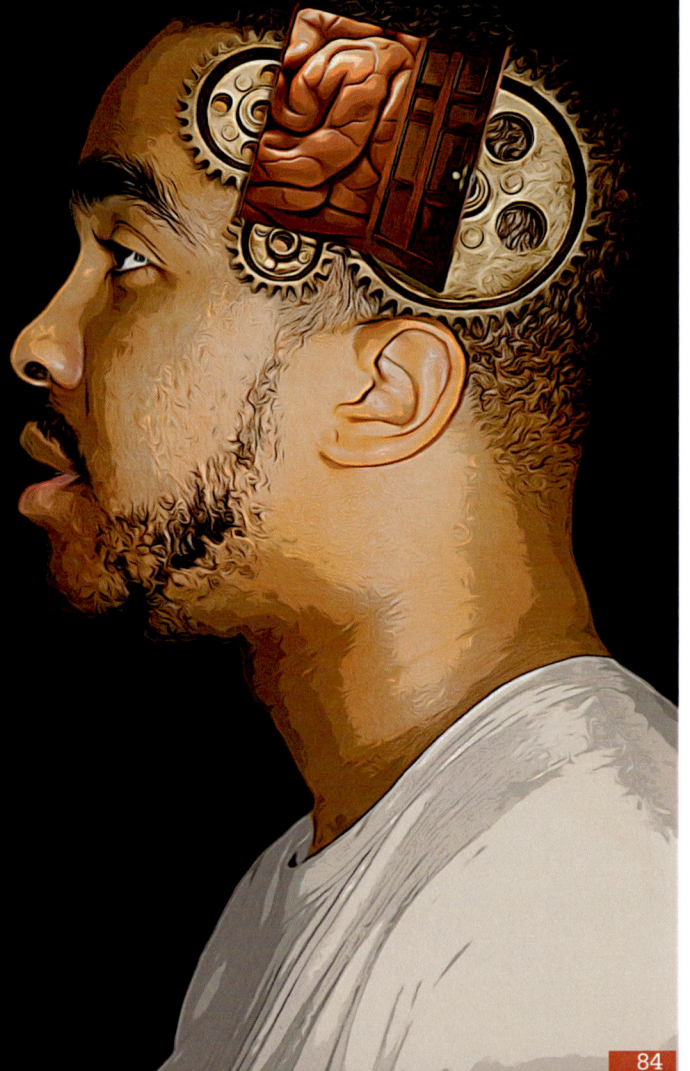

Each and every one of us wants to feel a sense of purpose, a sense of belonging, to be loved and accepted by others, and to be recognized for who we are and what we have accomplished—but America makes it difficult for us to achieve and sustain all of that. The system of oppression does not allow men of color to get too far out of the bucket before the elite pull us back down or contract our own kind to pull us back inside for them.

We are one mistake away from being fired from a job and we are one traffic violation and argument away from being killed or thrown in jail. Being jobless and the fear of death and incarceration (slavery) makes it difficult for us to find self-happiness, live purposeful lives, to provide for ourselves and our loved ones, and to take care of and manage our responsibilities which causes stress, anxiety, and depression. **We struggle to be happy! We struggle to survive!**

A verbal domestic dispute is recorded as Domestic Violence (DV) in some states. A colored man with a clean criminal record, who is accused of and has DV stamped on his fresh charging document is celebrated by the elite. Why? Because they make money each time a person is charged with a crime and each day a person is housed in their jails and prisons—I mean, a lot of money. Boys and men of color make up the majority of the population in jails and prisons in America.

In many cases, many women of color have falsified police reports stating their boyfriend or husband put his hands on her when he hadn't lifted a finger. Many falsified reports because they found him cheating, or because he left her for another woman, or various other reasons. Such reports led many innocent and successful men of color to a life of incarceration, losing everything they worked hard for because of the uncon trolled minds and behaviors of the women they were involved with.

The elite love when women of color work with them to destroy the lives that we (men of color) have created. That is why they contract many of our women through music, television shows, and other social factors that target the destruction of colored men. This kind of behavior is why I exercise extreme precaution when interacting with and choosing to be involved with women. All it takes is for one neighbor or bystander to witness me arguing with a woman in an aggressive manner before I'm shipped off to the county jail. So, in order for me to avoid incarceration and risk losing everything I have worked hard for, it is a must that I continue to avoid relationships with broken women, maintain my poise, ignore and walk away from all confrontations. **Come correct, or do not come at all!**

I have learned to spot the enemy from afar and to ignore their negative influences, those that can cost me everything that I built.

There are men who deserve to be punished for physically harming women, and there are women who deserve to be punished for assisting police officers in placing shackles on the wrists of men who are not guilty of physically harming them. What bothers me about this system of oppression—that deprives innocent colored men of rewarding lives—is that all women have to do is pick up a phone and lie to the authorities about her boyfriend or husband harming her, and his life is over. Police officers will pick him up, ask her to generate a police report, and then take the innocent brother into custody.

Also, what I do not like about the system is that whether a guy has put his hands on a woman or not, she isn't required to share her involvement. All she has to do is state what he allegedly did to her, and it becomes: The State of Ohio vs John Doe, not Jane Doe vs John Doe. There are many guys who provoke violence with women and there are also guys who are provoked by violent women, and both should be punished for their involvement. In cases where women have allegedly lied about being harmed and an innocent man goes to jail, the alleged victim should be required to take the stand during the criminal proceeding and forced to present her facts of the case: "proof beyond a reasonable doubt."

Since his freedom is on the line, and it is worse to convict an innocent person than to allow a guilty person to go free, her freedom should be placed on the line as well.

Being an innocent man of color charged with and or convicted of Domestic Violence denies us many opportunities to advance in life. In fact, a verbal Domestic Violence is not stated Verbal Domestic Violence on the initial charging document, it's simply written as Domestic Violence. Because of the stigma that comes with the label, when jobs, schools, banks, and organizations run our criminal background check and find Domestic Violence on our record, their initial thought is going to be: **"he beat on women."** and they would immediately deny us the opportunity we are requesting. Having no job, no money, no car, no home, no woman, and a criminal record means, **back to the ghetto we go,** with anyone who will allow us to sleep on their couch or floor.

Being a man of color housed back in impoverished environments—similar to the ones we previously escaped from—forces us to go back into survival mode, and develop animal-like instincts. We are forced to become a predator: stealing, robbing, burglarizing, and victimizing innocent people and businesses in order to survive. **We are forced to be preyed upon by other predators** who look like us, until either of us are buried in the ground or escorted to the impound.

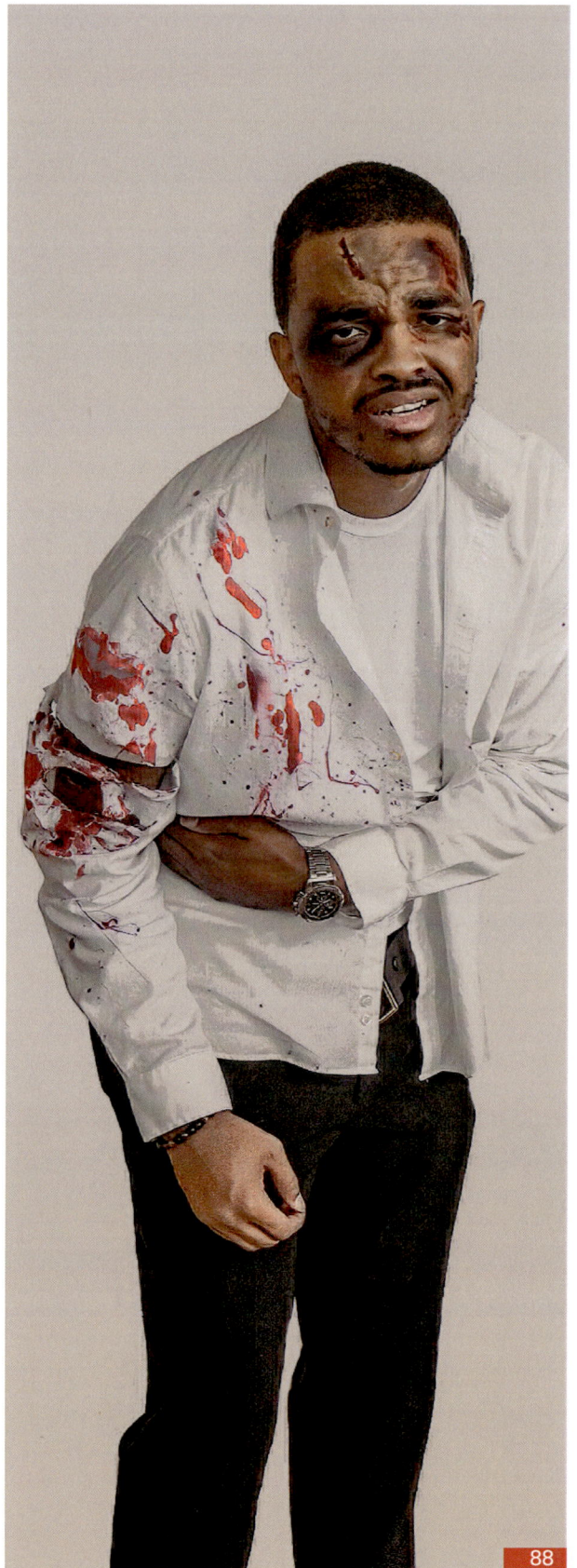

The fear of poverty, fear of incarceration, fear of death, and the fear of criticism, stress, anxiety, and depression were the many reasons why I lacked intimacy and sex in my relationships. Not because I was **"Fucking Another Bitch."**

So many of us suffer in silence and feel hopeless about the future because it seems like we cannot escape the harsh realities of life. There seems to be no freedom after following the North Star. Because there seems to be no escape, many of us turn to drugs, alcohol, and sex to cope with the mental and emotional pain we are experiencing. We are suffering from PTSD (Psychic Traumatic Slavery Disorder) that mental health professionals aren't able to cure us from, let alone able to help us cope with. Many of the women I was involved with, were not aware of or did not understand the demons I was battling and were unaware of the trapped corners everywhere I went in America. Many did not know because I was afraid to share what I was going through and because they never cared to know. They were only focused on their own feelings, emotions, responsibilities, problems, fame, and glamor, in which they were not able to recognize that I was suffering in silence. They had not discovered their woman powers to detect issues that bothered me. They did not have a mother's instinct to detect and nurture.

Author NeeNee Marie

Oftentimes, when I attracted a woman who I thought would assist me in getting free from Hell on Earth, she ended being just as bad as our oppressors: intentionally and unintentionally attempting to give me back to our slave owners whose plantations I had already avoided, because of the trauma and social influences she was affected by.

We (men) are not going to be affectionate or intimate with the woman we are involved with if something is bothering us that has to do with our fear of failing, finances, incarceration, racism, death, destructive criticism, or if our women are not doing anything to assist us in feeling better. Ladies, your looks are not enough, your sex is not enough, your meals are not enough, and your housekeeping is not enough, although we are very grateful for it all. We need you to play the Operation Game on our mind, body, and spirit, so we can better assist ourselves, you, our families, and our communities. So we can successfully continue the advancement of our race, in which the elite is trying desperately to prevent us from doing.

Verdi Photography

Ladies, when we are working on ourselves trying to reach certain milestones in life, or when we are in a lost or very emotional state and our intimacy and sex with you becomes limited, it is your job to assist us in feeling and becoming better versions of ourselves. Your nur-

turing and support is necessary at this time. If you have not been doing so already, it's important that you study our behaviors to identify if something is bothering us or not. If you identify a problem that may be affecting us and causing us to become distant from your love and affection, it is important that you figure out how to get us to share with you what is bothering us. Not criticize us about "Fucking Another Woman."

Once you gain our trust and we reveal the skeletons in our closet to you, it is imperative that you **DO NOT** disclose it with anyone: not your girlfriends, not your parents, **NOT ANYONE.**

However, you do have my permission to share the skeletons I have shared with you in this book. We all look for the women in our lives to be our confidant, who will save us from embarrassment, public humiliation, and criticism. If we discover that you have dis closed our personal information,- you may never fully gain our trust again. If and when we happen to reveal the skeletons in our closet to you, please try to work toward catering to our needs. Help us heal! We need you, just as much as you need us.

"A woman who does not make a man's problems hers, is a woman who will soon be without a man; a man who does not make a woman's problems his, is a man who will soon be without a woman."

This seems to be the reality for the majority of people nowadays. Many men and women are who and where they are in life because no one wants to make another person's problems theirs, or help them heal their open wounds. I have learned on my personal journey that sometimes we have to step outside of ourselves and shine the operating room light on others, preparing them for surgery. When we are so caught up in ourselves,

we lose sight of the people who are in need—their needs, wants, and desires. We receive a person in their good state and drive them to a bad state because we have failed to respond to their needs appropriately, and because we may have imposed our pain and trauma onto them, making them pay for something they had nothing to do with.

As I referenced earlier, a young child is unable to explain what he is feeling or why he is feeling a certain way when something is wrong, but in most cases his mother knows what he needs when he is whiny. As adults, many of us have seemed to have lost that kind of spiritual connection with adult-on-adult interactions. We cannot assume someone is OK when they respond with, "I'm OK" when we ask them how they are feeling. We have to pay attention to their tone of voice and body language as well. Many people who are suffering in silence hide behind their beautiful smile because they are afraid of what they are really fee ling getting out into the real world. They are afraid of destructive criticism and public humiliation, so they suffer in silence instead of seeking assistance.Most people who have committed suicide had been suffering in silence, hiding behind their beautiful smiles. We have to go beneath the surface of a person's words and smile—which involves observation of behavior—and help them heal the best way we know how: refer them to a specialist or work with them at their side.

As I mentioned earlier, I did not allow the women in on what I was really experiencing internally because society had programmed me to never show a sign of weakness: **if I did, then I was weak. I was not a man.** The truth was, keeping my emotions and the things that bothered me inside, made me weak and less of a man, because doing so affected my behavior and relationships with others. **I felt as if I was being eaten alive.**

Releasing my anger and frutration and sharing my experiences with others in a positive way made me stronger. Getting Completely Naked helped shape me into a man. By doing so, it has allowed me to receive true love, joy, intimacy, respect, and kindness. It has also allowed me to achieve my goals and desires and assist others with healing and becoming the best version of themselves.

I did not want to leave you herewithout sharing with you the origin of our pain. But I must go.

However, if you come with me to the next chapter, I will undress the monsters that have caused us a great deal of pain--pain that many of us are currently walking around with today as a result of their horrific behavior.

Come On In ;

Find Out Who They Are.

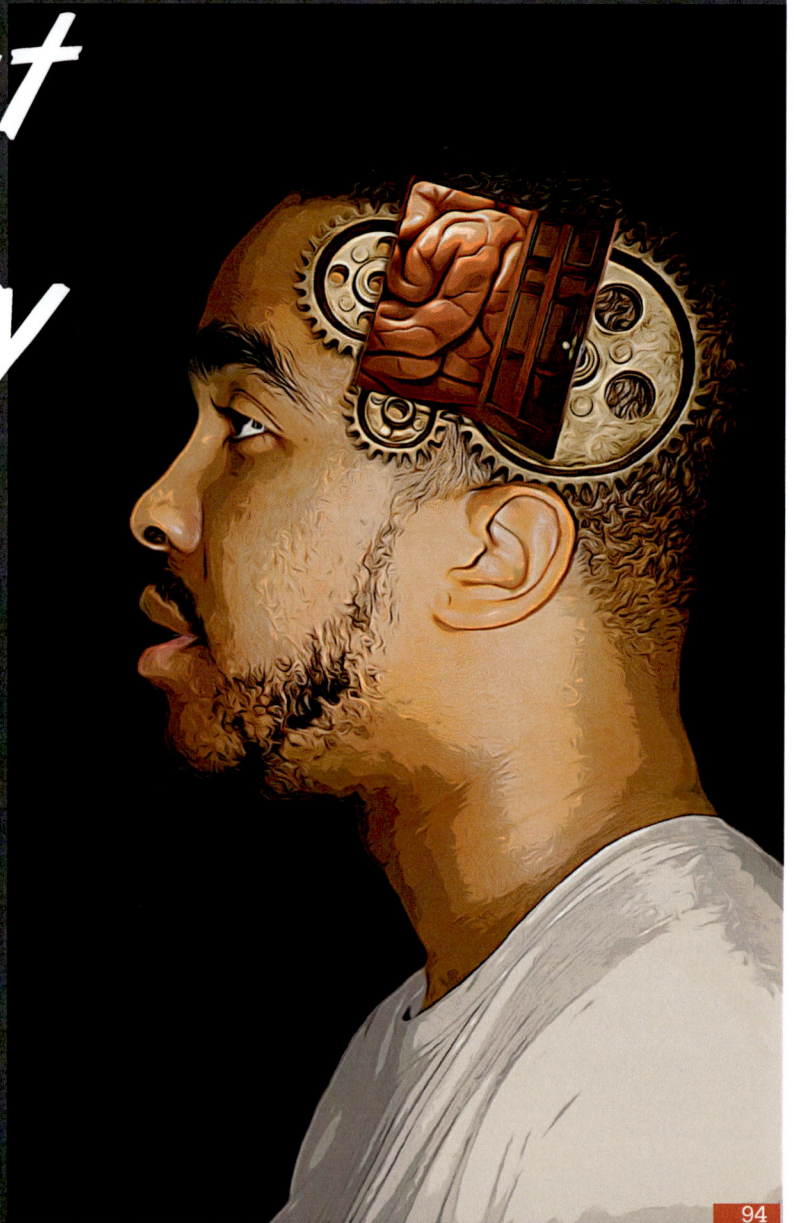

"GENERATIONAL CURSES, PTSD & THE PAIN MY FAMILY CAUSED ME"

Behind The Design

There are many people who do not know what it is like to be taken away from their homeland and their family, or what it is like to be robbed of their identity, knowledge, spirituality, language, history, and resources, or what it is like to be dehumanized by another race of people who forced them, their families, and millions of other people who were just like them to work over 400 years of free labor to build a nation they have no control in, and who have said to those of us who have families that experienced the horrific treatment: **"Slavery Was So Long Ago; Get Over It!"**

Fuck Them, Too. That shit does not feel good. It does NOT feel good at all.

Jameel Davis

Today, we all are still traumatized and affected by the pain and generational curses inflicted on our families from slavery. Trauma caused by slave owners like Willie Lynch and his Making of A Slave Teachings, that affect our ability to cope, love ourselves, love one another, learn effectively, and live dignified and beautiful lives. When my ancestors were kidnapped from their homeland by white men who had tricked them into being brought to the Americas—to live a life of captivity on what we know as slave plantations, to build the American economy we see today—they were tortured by those men as they worked day in and day out for over 400 years creating the American and other world economies. People of color have experienced the worst brutality in the history of mankind and still to this day, those of us who have come after them are affected by what they went through. We are still being treated worse than any other race of people.

For those who have told us to get over it because it was so long ago: slavery was not that long ago. On January 1, 1863, former United States President Abraham Lincoln issued the Emancipation Proclamation which supposedly abolished slavery. The proclamation declared "that all persons held as slaves" within the rebellious states "are, and henceforward shall be free." That was less than 160 years ago. It was not that long ago. And besides, 160 years is not enough time to overcome the Psychic Trauma the white race has caused us, especially while still being enslaved today. Yes, we are still enslaved by the white race. Stay with me.

Although Abraham Lincoln abolished slavery in the rebellious states, he did not abolish slavery entirely. Many people of color were still held captive on slave plantations long after the signing of the Emancipation Proclamation. The proclamation had supposedly declared us free from cruel and unusual punishment, but many white people refused to honor it by continuing to beat and lynch us, and many white people currently dishonor it because we are still being mistreated by them. Many still dishonor the Emancipation Proclamation by way of police brutality and the cruel and unusual punishment we experience in jails and prison systems today. We can agree that the proclamation was never intended for us to be free, but to be physically, mentally, emotionally, and spiritually enslaved forever, right?

We are still slaves in this country, and the 13th Amendment of the United States Constitution—which was passed by the Senate and House, and approved by President Lincoln for the amendment to be sent to the state legislatures—proves it.

In case you have not read it, the 13th Amendment reads: "...neither slavery nor involuntary servitude, **except as a punishment for** crime whereof the party shall have been duly convicted, shall exist within the United States, or any place subject to their jurisdiction." The 13th Amendment had abolished slavery in 1865, which was two years after the Emancipation Proclamation was signed, and the forefounders of slavery had already imposed sanctions for newly freed slaves who committed crimes: slaves who had already been robbed of their liberty by the forefounders of slavery, who approved the Emancipation Proclamation, who wrote the United States Constitution and the 13th Amendment, and who had slaves of their own. Such sanctions were imposed on newly freed slaves who had been denied resources, the opportunity to learn, to raise a family of their own, to develop skills that would help build our own economy or skills that would allow them to be self-sufficient. Many only had skills obtained from their forced labor on the plantations in which they lived.

The 14th and the 15th Amendment of the United States Constitution was supposed to be in place to protect the rights of people of color. The 14th Amendment guaranteed us citizenship and promised that the federal government would enforce "equal protection of the laws." The 15th Amendment stated that no one could be denied the right to vote based on "race, color or previous condition of servitude." The federal government does not enforce the equal protection of laws, and the people of color who are convicted of a felony crime are denied the right to vote.

Although we have been granted citizenship in this country, there is no liberty and justice for our people because the ones who enslaved us to begin with (and their children, and their children's children) are **the ones who make and enforce the laws that our people must follow or be put back into slavery (jails and prisons) as the 13th Amendment states.**

Who is going to punish them for what they have done and what they currently are doing to us?

3KP Marketing

Many people want us to get over slavery and the effects of it, as if there are resources available to reverse 400 years of psychic trauma, the worst trauma anyone could ever imagine. Trauma far worse than what our soldiers and their families have experienced during their tour of deployment fighting wars. The white race had a 400-year head start and that is why many white people and other races who are not affected by slavery are able to fix their mouth to tell us to get over it.

Telling us to get over slavery is like telling former United States soldiers to get over the civil wars that nearly cost them their life, and the lives of their battle buddies who they depended on. It is like telling families to get over their loved ones who were killed and or injured in battle. Telling us to get over slavery is like telling people who witnessed bodies drop to the ground from the World Trade Center, to get over September 11, 2001 and nearly 3000 people who were killed.

If you are not a person of color and are not affected by the conditions of slavery, I would like to take you on a short journey of what slave catchers and slave owners did to my ancestors, how their horrific actions influenced the negative behavior of my family today, and how my family's behavior affected me. After this journey, I welcome you to tell me what you would have done to prevent such behaviors if it was you and your family, and what you could do today to reverse the conditions of your people if they were affected by slavery.

Come On In ;

Do Not

Be

Afraid.

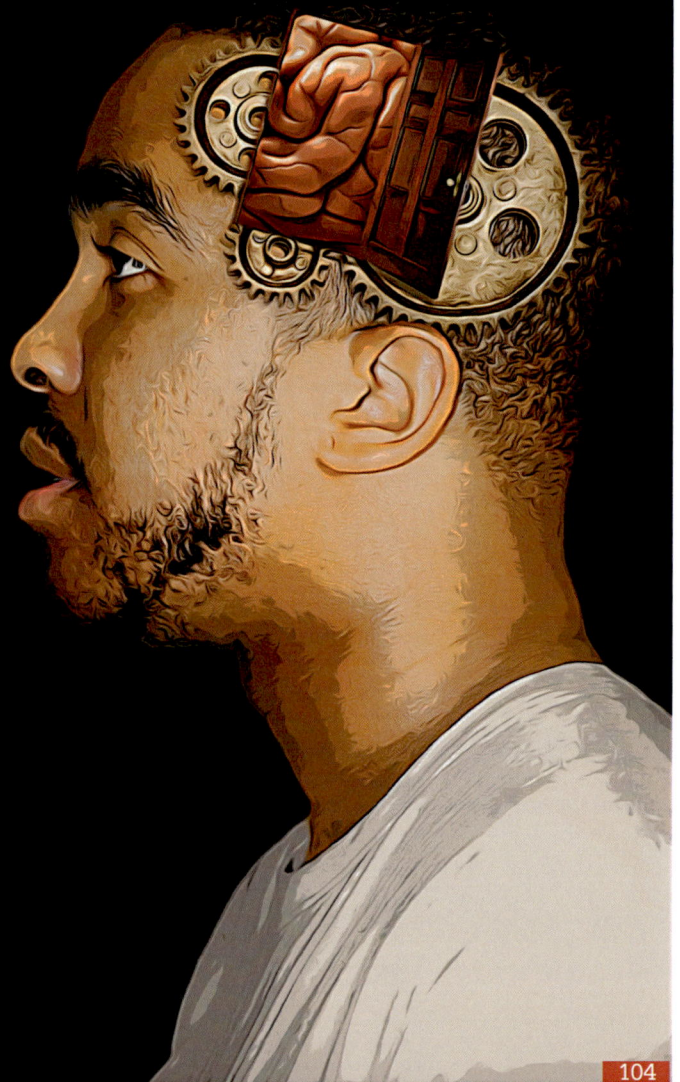

> The conditions of one generation becomes the condition of the next generation, and the actions of one generation becomes the history of the next.

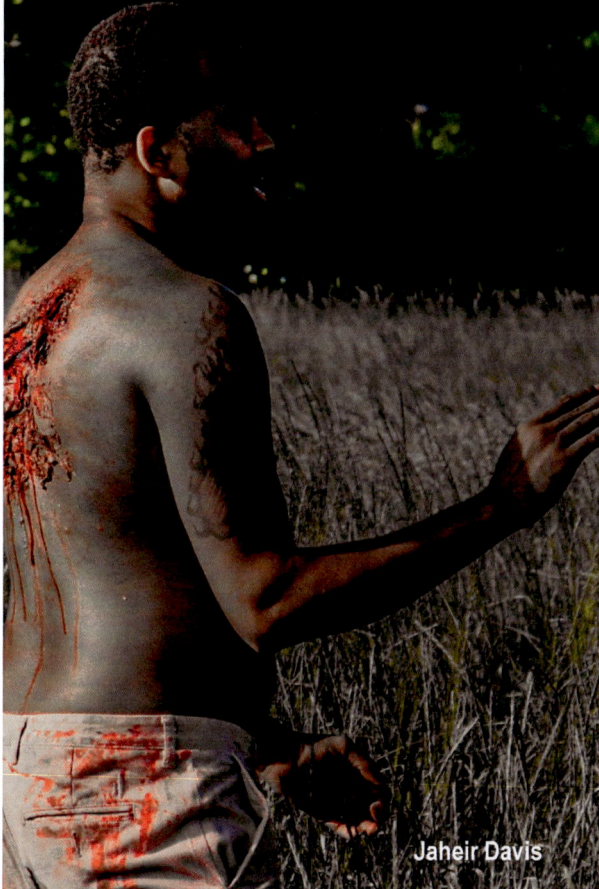

Jaheir Davis

My family who were once a very strong, self-loving, charming, compassionate, disciplined, highly educated, wealthy, and highly skilled group of people were whipped, beaten, shackled, and escorted by white slave catchers to ships that transported them from their homes and villages in West Africa, across the Atlantic ocean, to America, Brazil, Cuba, Middle Eastern countries and the Caribbean Islands. Some of the strongest men in my family were captured by slave catchers while they were out gathering food for the village. Once captured, they were brought back to the villages where they lived and beaten in front of women and children who were resisting capture by other slave catchers.

When the women in my family saw the leaders and protectors of our families and villages in shackles, unable to fight back and to protect them, they had no choice but to surrender themselves and their children to the slave catchers. As they arrived at shore, where all other captured villagers had been stationed, they witnessed captured villagers being separated from their families and forced onto big ships, as they waited their turn. The men in my family at tempted to fight back but could not succeed because they were outnumbered. Eventually, they were harmed even more and separated from their families. Children were snatched out of their mother's arms, and they all boarded different ships (blessed by church leaders from England) that took them to different parts of the world where they would never see their loved ones again. Can you imagine yourself in their shoes?

When my family arrived to their slave owner's (those who had purchased them) plantation—whether it was in America, Brazil, Cuba, Middle Eastern countries, or in the Caribbean Islands, they had no way of getting in contact with those who were separated from them. All they had was other West Africans who had been captured and brought along with them. Those men, women, and children who were in captivity on the plantations with them were not of the same village as them. Not even the same country. They were all from different countries and villages which made it difficult for them to converse with one another. This system was done intentionally so they could not work together to escape, and so slave owners could eventually turn them against one another. Slave owners were beginning to break my family physically, mentally, emotionally, and spiritually.

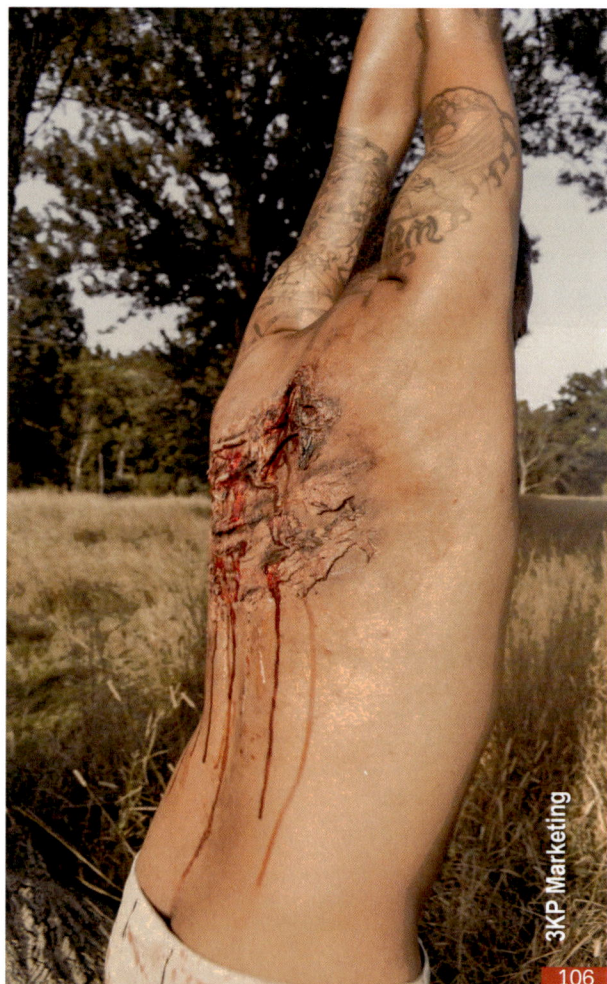

My family was forced to forget their African names. Slave owners had beaten it out of them, and they were given new names by their slave owners. My family was forced to adopt the English language and was beaten every time they spoke in their native tongue. Although they were forced to adopt the English language, they were not allowed to read or write it. Those who got caught were nearly beaten to death and killed. My family scattered throughout America, Brazil, Cuba, Middle Eastern countries, and throughout the Caribbean Islands were beaten if they prayed to their ancestors or practiced any spiritual rituals from Africa and the countries they came from. They were forced to adopt the religion of the land in which they had arrived.

With the African Slave Trade, my family was born into Islam. My family that was brought to America, Brazil, Cuba, and the Caribbean were taught Christianity by Europe-ans and the Catholic church. My family was forced to forget their history, and everything regarding their history had been destroyed.

When my family disobeyed their slave owners or messed up, they were beaten in front of all the other people who were slaves, that allowed slave owners to use fear and distrust to control my family. This harsh treatment put the fear of God and distrust in my family and all the other people on the plantation. Slave owners knew that all men and women on their plantation would just stand around and watch as another colored man or woman was tortured and killed by them. They knew they would not do anything to help the person in need out of fear for being next. Slave owners knew the women in my family would grow to no longer rely on men for protection after witnessing the strongest men get tortured and killed. Slave owners knew men would eventually lose their trust in women, women would lose their trust in men, and children would lose trust in their parents, and everyone would lose trust in everyone who looked like them.

Author NeeNee Marie

Author NeeNee Marie

Slave owners knew that if they broke my family how they broke their horses, we would be conditioned and controlled by white slave owners for many years to come. Former slave owner Willie Lynch mentioned in his Making of A Slave Letter: distrust is stronger than trust and envy stronger than adulation, respect, or admiration. He continued by saying that people of color, after receiving this indoctrination (brainwashing), shall carry on and will become self-refueling and self-generating for hundreds of yearsmaybe thousands. He made it clear that during the indoctrination of my family, that it was necessary that we trust and depend on our slave owners and not each other: that we must love, respect, and trust only them.

In order for slave owners to break my family, they had to break them like they broke the horses they rode—taking them from their natural state where they had the natural ability to take care of their young, and breaking them into a new natural state of dependency.

Slave owners knew that my family was dangerous in their natural state...even in captivity, because they had a tendency to get to freedom. Slave owners knew they could not get my family to work in their natural state and therefore had to break their will to resist. In order to make that happen, slave owners took the meanest and most restless men in my family and stripped them of their clothing. They did so in front of the other males, females, and infant children. After stripping the men of their clothing, slave owners tied each of their legs to a different horse faced in the opposite direction, tarred, and feathered them, set them on fire, and beat both horses to pull them apart—all in front of my other family members. What the slave owners did next: they took a bullwhip and beat the remaining males to the point of death, in front of the women and children.

They put the fear of God in my family.

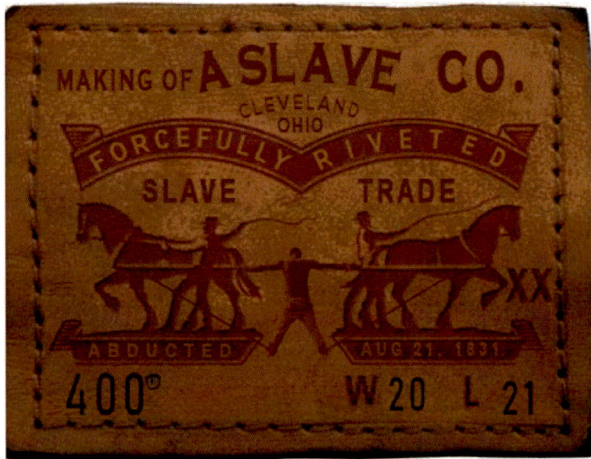

Author NeeNee Marie / Kensho (Graphic Designer)

What this brutalization and indoctrination did to the women in my family was, reverse their natural state of being psychologically dependent, by being forced to watch their slave owners kill and torture the meanest and mentally strongest men (and all other males) in their presence. This forced the women to be left alone, unprotected, and with the image of a strong protective male destroyed. As a result of the male image removed from their natural psychological state, they were broken from their natural state of colored male dependency, to a frozen psychologically independent state.

In their new psychologically independent state, the women "naturally" raised their sons and daughters in reversed roles. For fear of their sons being killed and brutalized by their slave owners, they psychologically trained them to be physically strong, but mentally weak and dependent on them for guidance and survival. The women then trained their daughters to be psychologically frozen and independent just like them.

What this did to the other men in my family was make them fearful of their slave owners, mentally weak, and dependent on their mothers as their slave owners had intended, therefore putting the women out in front and the men in the back scared, depending on their mother and other women for protection. Reverse psychology.

Jameel Davis

My family, in their natural state, were dangerous, and had the tendency to kill slave owners in order to be set free. Before my family had been broken like horses, slave owners had to be alert at all times out of fear of losing their lives to the people in my family. Slave owners having to be on alert did not allow them to sleep at night or work effectively and efficiently on their global economic plans. Knowing that the men in my family were the meanest, strongest, and most restless, they knew the breaking process would allow them to rest at night and get work done in the morning. They knew by reversing the natural state of the men and women in my family, women would stand guard for them while they slept and worked, and the men would stand behind the women scared to act like they did before they were broken.

Slave owners knew that if they continued to break the natural state of my family, putting the women deeper into a frozen state of independence, and by killing the strong and protective male image—forcing the men into a dependent state that their cycle of reverse psychology and psychic trauma would be on cruise control for hundreds of years or more.

In order for slave owners to keep the cycle spinning on an axis with no intentions of slowing down, they forced the young female children—who had watched the brutalization of the men who had grown of age to reproduce children of their own—to mate with young male childr who had watched the brutaliza-tion of the men who had come of age to reproduce children. After mating, the men were then taken from their families and the women were forced to keep moving and working, therefore, allowing more men in my family to become mentally weak, hiding behind women, while women stayed out in front, learning, becoming smarter, and protecting her slave owners, while psychologically training her young for the next cycle.

3KP Marketing

It is now year 2021, 309 years after Willie Lynch's Making of A Slave, 158 years after President Lincoln signed the Emancipation Proclamation, and 156 years after the 13th Amendment was passed by state legislatures, and many of my family members who came after my ancestors who were in chattel slavery, are still traumatized and affected by Willie Lynch's horrific teachings. They are still in their reversed psychological state, rotating on an ongoing psychologically dependent and frozen independent axis as Willie Lynch knew they would be, 309 years ago.

Many of the men and young men in my family are still unable to gain the necessary knowledge to be self-sufficient or take care of their family, because they are psychologically dependent and still denied the opportunity to sit at the top of the food chain. Willie Lynch and many other slave owners who were like him, knew this day would come where millions of men of color would still be walking around physically strong, but mentally weak. They knew that millions of boys would naturally fall behind in school, end up on the streets, and live a life of criminal activity until they were buried in the ground or captured and taken back to slavery (jails and prisons) as they stated in 1712 and in the 13th Amendment of the United States Constitution in 1865.

I mentioned in Chapter Two, Finding The Love of A Black Man, that Mansfield B. Frazier stated:

"Many single mother homes don't have a foundation of academic and economic education, "Many single mother homes don't have a foundation of academic and economic education, intimacy, compassion, love and respect. As a result, young boys fall behind in school, become distant from love and affection from women, and eventually end up on the streets, fostering a life of drugs, alcohol, and criminal activity, in which many end up in the jail and prison system."

Slave owners knew the number of absent men of color in black households would increase at an alarming rate as the years went by, because they broke men from our natural state of being into a new broken state that we believe is normal.

Many men of color are becoming more psychologically dependent and because they lack self-sufficiency, many women of color are becoming more psychologically independent— they are becoming increasingly physically and emotionally dependent on white men because they can't depend on men of color to lead, provide for, and protect them or their children.

Many men are jobless, hiding behind their mothers and other women who are protecting them from the evilness of society, while their mothers, women, and daughters are out in front: unprotected, learning, achieving, and attempting to achieve their goals and desires. The reverse roles implemented 300 years ago are still in full effect. **Destroy their mind, keep the body.**

While many men are dependent on women to provide the necessities for survival, many women are dependent on government systems (white men) to provide for them, their children, and the men who are dependent on them. Because women are dependent on systems like housing assistance, men of color are legally not allowed to live with a woman who has government (white men) assistance, like low-income housing. As a result of men not being able to live in the home with women and the children they have fathered, women in those environments grow to be angry and frustrated because of the limitations that come with their environment (loneliness, poverty, violence, and the lack of resources to get her children out of that environment). Because they are angry with their circumstances especially because of the absence of their father, their children's father, and a strong black male image they are naturally and secretly attracting men into their home who are psychologically dependent and emotionally needy: who reflect the behaviors of their father and children's father. They are just dressed in a different costume.

These men are their intoxicants; they are their drug. After coming back down from their high back to their natural state of anger, frustration, depression, and anxiety they send the mentally weak men packing because they legally are not supposed to be there, and because they are unable to provide anything other than sex to temporarily numb their pain. Many end up getting pregnant by these men.

These same women shelter their sons, attempting to protect them from being like their fathers or the men they have dated, out of fear of losing him to violence or to incarceration. While in shelter, their mothers are screaming in their faces, beating them for making messes, threatening them for disturbing their rest or phone conversations, and daring them to cry when they are hurting. These mothers call them derogatory names (the same names Hip Hop artists use to degrade less fortunate men) and slap them around in public.

At home, their sons are forced to suffer in silence after their mothers force them to be quiet after she harms them physically, mentally, and emotionally. Mothers ignore their needs to be nurtured and held and allow others to harm him to make him tough.

These same mothers cover their wounds with fine clothing, shoes, jewelry, and electronics, to show him off in public and get praised for being a great mother. And people wonder why many black men from single mother households cheat.

"No Woman on this Planet is better than his mother! No matter how good a woman may be, Black men subconsciously believe somewhere inside her exists the same terrible characteristics of his mother."

-- Ms. Melanian.

Daughters of these vicious, man eating mothers grow up to be angry just like them: psychologically dependent on the system. They grow older to attract and mate with guys who are similar to their fathers, the men their mothers have dated (and who are similar to the men their mothers have raised), thus keeping the vicious cycle of psychological oppression Willie Lynch imposed on beautiful people of color less than 309 years ago on autopilot.

"ALL BROKEN PEOPLE WHO ARE IN ARELATIONSHIP WITH SOMEONE CHEATS, ENTERTAINS THE THOUGHT OF CHEATING, AND WILL EVENTUALLY CHEAT! "

Show me a broken person in a relationship and I'll show you a person who cheated, entertains cheating, and who is thinking about cheating.

During my earlier years (I am 30 years old writing this), the pain I endured, my behavior toward the women I was involved with because of the pain, and the pain my parents endured and their behavior toward me, was a result of the Willie Lynch Syndrome. Learning my history and about the Making of A Slave, I am able to see why distrust is still stronger than trust, and envy stronger than adulation, respect, or admiration in my family. I have managed to reprogram my mind to its natural state of psychological independence and have made my way to the front, guarding myself and others from being attacked in our sleep.This has allowed me to achieve almost everything I set forth to achieve. Doing so caused many people in my immediate family (who are still on the Willie Lynch autopilot) to distrust and be envious of me, instead of having respect and admiration for the positive things I stand for: positivity, happiness, and programming our minds to our natural state so we can try to overcome the Post Traumatic Slave Disorders caused by the white race, and plant fruitful seeds in the minds of those who come after us so they can go on and live dignified and beautiful lives.

My family does not support my work, and that shit does not feel good. It does NOT feel good at all. I have something to get off my chest about the pain they have caused me.

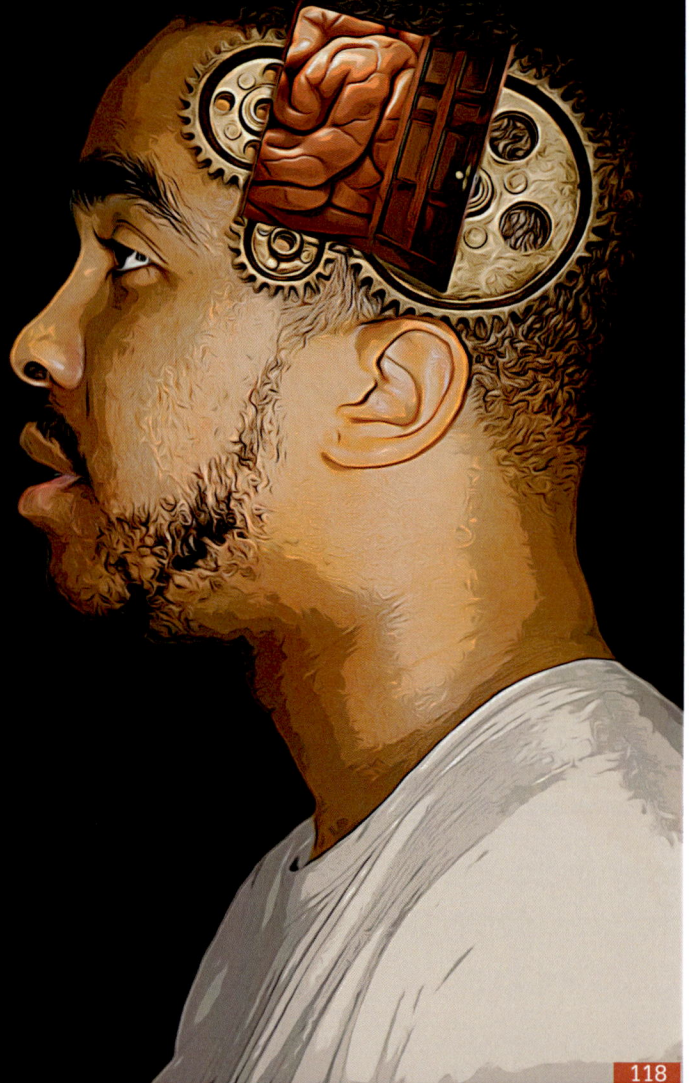

Come On In ;

And See What

I Have

To Say.

Dear Family,

I understand your pain and suffering, how negativity has overpowered your consciousness, and how you only support and cater to things that are negative, but feel so good to you as a result. I am on a positive wave right now and have been on it for quite some time, in an effort to reverse generational curses that have affected the behaviors of our family and society. I know you do not support the positive and good things I produce and stand for, and that is perfectly fine. I am no longer upset with you because I know why you don't. However, your absence is the reason I have become the man I am today.

I no longer wish to hear how proud of me you are, and I no longer wish to receive your congratulations unless your behavior changes. Reason being, my work has not made an impact on you in a positive way, and because many of you have sat back and watched me struggle to get where I am now, while you supported drugs, alcohol and other people in our family who lived (and currently live) a life of negativity and criminal activity. If I made a positive impact on your life, you would not still be on a low vibration, soaking up negative energy—energy that is preparing the next generation in our family for failure. Let that sink in!

Instead, you would be working with me to help reverse the conditions of pain and defeat our family and race have faced for the past 400 years. Family, although we may not see eye to eye, and you may be afraid to change for the better, I want you to know that I still love you, but I must keep my distance from you. I am pure and negativity is the cause of disease, destruction, and disaster. I will continue to progress forward the best way I know how. I wish you all the best.

Jameel

"The more a foreigner knows about the language of another country, the more he is able to move through all levels of that society. Therefore, if the foreigner is an enemy of the country, to the extent that he knows the body of the language, to that extent is the country vulnerable to attack or invasion of a foreign culture. If you take a slave, if you teach him all about your language, he will know all your secrets, and he is then no more a slave, for you can't fool him any longer."

- Willie Lynch

I have learned the language of the foreign country in which I reside, therefore I am no fool. And although I am no fool, I am still one mistake away from getting fired and one argument, violation, and accusation away from being buried in the ground or locked behind the walls of the jails and prisons built by the families of the founding fathers of slavery.

Lets Break These Curses.

Author NeeNee Marie

Jameel Davis

Jameel Davis

121

Jameel Davis

Listen To "White"

04 CHAPTER FOUR

"MINUTE MAN"

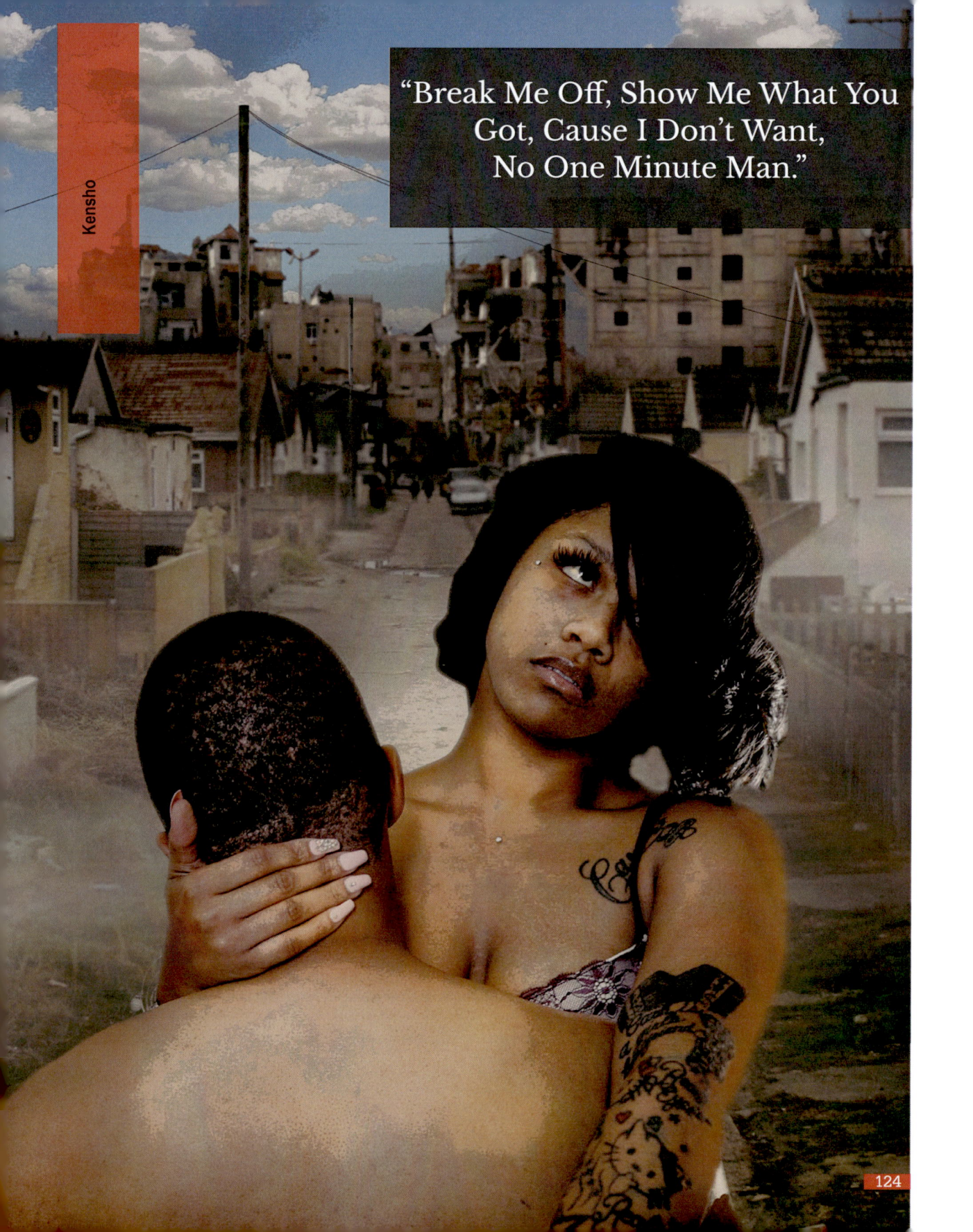

"Break Me Off, Show Me What You Got, Cause I Don't Want, No One Minute Man."

There is another fear that comes with being a black man, and that is the fear of not being able to please a woman mentally, emotionally, spiritually, financially, and most importantly, physically (sexually). I remember being the minute man Missy Elliott quoted not wanting in her song. There were many times I could not last longer than a minute, no matter how hard I tried to keep my mind off ejaculating. There were times I had stage fright (could not get it up) no matter how beautiful the woman was. Not being able to please the women I had been with in all their desired areas of need (especially sexually), killed every bit of self-esteem and self-confidence I had in my adolescent and early adult years. I could not save myself the self-embarrassment of finishing way faster than expected, and not being able to get an erection for the beautiful women my dick seemed to not be physically attracted to.

There are many guys who are publicly and privately shamed by women they were and are currently sexually involved with for their "short cummings." Also, there are many guys who perform well in bed, who were caught cheating, and who have been lied on about and publicly shamed for having a small penis, by women they have cheated on. Many of those women formed lies out of hurt and attempted to publicly humiliate them so other women would not be sexually attracted to them... or maybe just to protect other women from experiencing a similar pain. Although I had never been publicly shamed and never brought to trial by the women I was involved with for my sprints, I was still upset for not being able to satisfy women like I had seen male pornography stars satisfy the women they were with on their sex tapes.

I do remember being lied on about having a small dick lol! One of the females I was sexually involved with planted the "don't mess with him, he has a small dick" bug in the ears of other females who were openly interested in me, after my best friend at the time who she was also sexually involved with at the time and I arrived at her home and played a trick on her. She had her cake (him) and ate it (me) too. She did not know we were friends. I was not embarrassed by the bug she had planted because I was very confident with the size of my dick and because she only did it out of pain caused by her own embarrassment. The whole ordeal with her was funny, because my best friend and I always talked about females we had been with, and when this particular female came up, we planned a set up by playing the R. Kelly & Usher "Same Girl" trick on her. The only difference was, she was not a twin. She was literally the same girl. The elephant in the room was addressed...and after we left, the bug had been killed.

JP Films

127

During my adolescence and early adult years, there were times where I felt I was barely making it count in the bedroom; I can still see some of the expressions on the faces of women after not being able to get aroused at the time of sex, and after being knocked out early in the first round when I did lol! Although I was knocked down early, many times in the first round, for the most part I was able to get back up and fight again...a few times getting knocked right back out...lol!. The vaginas of those women just felt that good—I could not keep from ejaculating quickly. I had no self-control. When I was cheating, I often finished quickly out of fear of getting caught and after having those "I should not be doing this" thoughts.

I mentioned in Chapter Two, Finding the Love of a Black Man, that many of the women I was involved with were just my intoxicants, helping me cope with the pain and demons I was battling at the time; they were a quick, temporary fix to my problems. They were the Tylenol to my headaches. I do not mean this in a way of disrespect because I have never—and will never—disrespect a woman's body. Whenever I had sex with them, being in the moment took my mind off whatever was bothering me; their sex numbed my pain.

I was never a hit it and quit it kind of guy, but more of a one-night stand kind of guy, with women who were involved with a guy they hated, but could not walk away from. We were drugging each other. Because I was still affected by traumas, my migraines would return, and I needed more Tylenol. I did not learn this until after my re-evaluation period I told you about in Chapter Two.

After experiencing premature ejaculation (PE) for quite some time, I thought it was normal for young men to finish quickly. I thought I had to wait until I turned thirty years old before I would be able to last longer during sex. I was wrong! It was not normal for guys my age to finish quickly, and I did not have to wait until I was thirty before I could last longer in bed. At age twenty-five, I learned there are many men—both older and younger—who suffer from PE and who are afraid of speaking with others (even their doctors) about it.

I had been having sex for eleven years and was never taught how to properly have sex (satisfy a woman) other than how to use a condom. I was never taught about PE or erectile dysfunction (ED). It took me eleven years to research (via Google) my symptoms and to build up the courage to share what I had been experiencing during sex with my Caucasian female physician. During an annual physical, I decided to get it off my chest. After she completed her examination and my assessment, I told her I suffered from PE and asked if there was anything she could do to help. This is when I found out my short sprints were a result of health complications. My doctor told me I was finishing sooner than I expected because I was experiencing anxiety, stress, and depression.

Whatever was bothering me was in the way of me performing my best in bed. I was battling those same demons. I asked her if there was a cure for PE; she said she would prescribe me Citalopram and that it would treat my depression and anxiety. After further research, I learned the medication she prescribed me was given to patients battling **clinical depression**—a mental health disorder characterized by a persistently depressed mood or loss of interestin activities, causing significant impairment in daily life obsessive **compulsive disorder** excessive thoughts (obsessions) that lead to repetitive behaviors (com pulsions) and **social anxiety disorder** a chronic mental health condition in which social interactions cause irrational anxiety. Everyday social interactions caused me to have irrational anxiety, fear, self-consciousness, and embarrassment. I was still suffering from the psychic slave trauma that slave owners imposed on my family hundreds of years ago.

After taking Citalopram for the first time, I did not feel well at all; I was dizzy, lightheaded, nauseous, and was breathing rapidly. I was sick. I informed my physician of the side effects from the medication and she said it was because the dosage was too high. She said she would prescribe me a lower dosage. I tried the lower dosage and the side effects were just as bad. After those moments of illness I decided I would no longer rely on medicine to help cure my PE. I informed my physician that I would no longer be taking them as a crutch. I realized my physician did not have my mental health in her best interest, and was not telling me the truth about Citalopram curing me of PE. I believe she told me the medicine would cure me from PE because I was young and incompetent and knew I would rely on the medicine to cope, therefore her getting more money from my health insurance provider.

I say this because she was not a mental health professional, did not give me a mental health assessment, and did not give me a psych referral to see a mental health professional. I simply told her I was suffering from PE and she just wrote me a prescription for Citalopram. As I mentioned earlier in Chapter Two, there are no treatment programs for people of color who are suffering from psychic traumatic slave disorder. Knowing that, I learned there is also no medicine that cures people from mental disorders, just medicine to help people temporarily cope until the medicine wears off, and it's time for them to take more.

After discontinuing Citalopram, I tried male enhancements displayed in local stores and given to me by male relatives. Those did not help either, instead they caused similar side effects like Citalopram. After experiencing the side effects of Citalopram and male enhancements, I decided I wanted to be able to satisfy a woman without the help of any supplements or enhancements. I did not want to cheat. **I wanted to satisfy her naturally.**

Author NeeNee Marie

Feeding my mind healthy positive things and environments people, places, images, and music during my re-evaluation period helped rid me of stress, anxiety, depression, and helped me achieve some of my personal goals. As I mentioned at the end of Chapter Three, negativity is the cause of disease, destruction, and disaster. Recognizing that I have perseverance, have overcome many of life's greatest challenges, and that I excel in almost every sport or activity I participate in, boosted my self-confidence and self-esteem. I knew that if I applied the same attitude and energy I put into achieving my goals, dreams, and excelling in activities I am great at into the bedroom... I would achieve my goal of naturally satisfying a woman. I would own the bedroom.

I realized that a positive mindset, discipline, exercise, and good eating habits play an important part in health, behavior, sports, and activities. In order for me to perform well in any sport, I have to have confidence that I can play, discipline to control my mind and body during play, be physically fit, eat food, and drink beverages that give me the required nutrients and energy needed to play that sport well.

Also, with sports like cross-county and swimming, it was important that I knew how to breathe properly. During my minute man years, I did not have confidence to perform well, a positive mindset, discipline to control my mind and body during sex, I did not workout, eat or breathe well, because of the stress, anxiety, and depression I was experiencing. I had been eating a lot of sodium-rich foods (which lead to high blood pressure), sugar (that leads to diabetes), and I was only drinking beverages that were rich in sugar. The food and beverages I was consuming were not foods that helped me perform well during sex. What I was consuming prevented adequate blood flow to my penis and adequate blood flow in the penis leads to a longer and stronger erection.

During my scheduled 5K cross-country and swim meets in the bedroom, I would rush into the vagina oftentimes without confidence, no control, holding my breath, and contracting my abdominal muscles, when I should have been in control of myself, breathing, and releasing those muscles. Rushing in without confidence and control while holding my breath, and contracting my abdominal muscles led to rapid orgasms, disqualifying me from the competitions. I did not know the rules; I was not prepared, and therefore I could not keep up. I tapped out in 60 seconds of what was supposed to be at least 35 minutes to hour-long competitions.

When I stopped eating foods that were rich in salt, decreased my meat intake, cut back on junk food and desserts, decreased my soft drink intake, stopped drinking Kool-Aid, started exercising, and strengthened my mind, body and spirit during my re-evaluation period, I saw a huge improvement during sex. I ate more of a plant-based diet, increased my vegetable, fruit, and water intake, which allowed blood to flow adequately to my penis for a longer and stronger erection. A healthy mind, body, and spirit was the medicine I needed to overcome stress, anxiety, depression, my shortcomings, and stage fright.

Author NeeNee Marie

Although I had enhanced my performance in the bedroom, I still had not mastered the art of sexually satisfying a woman.

JP Films

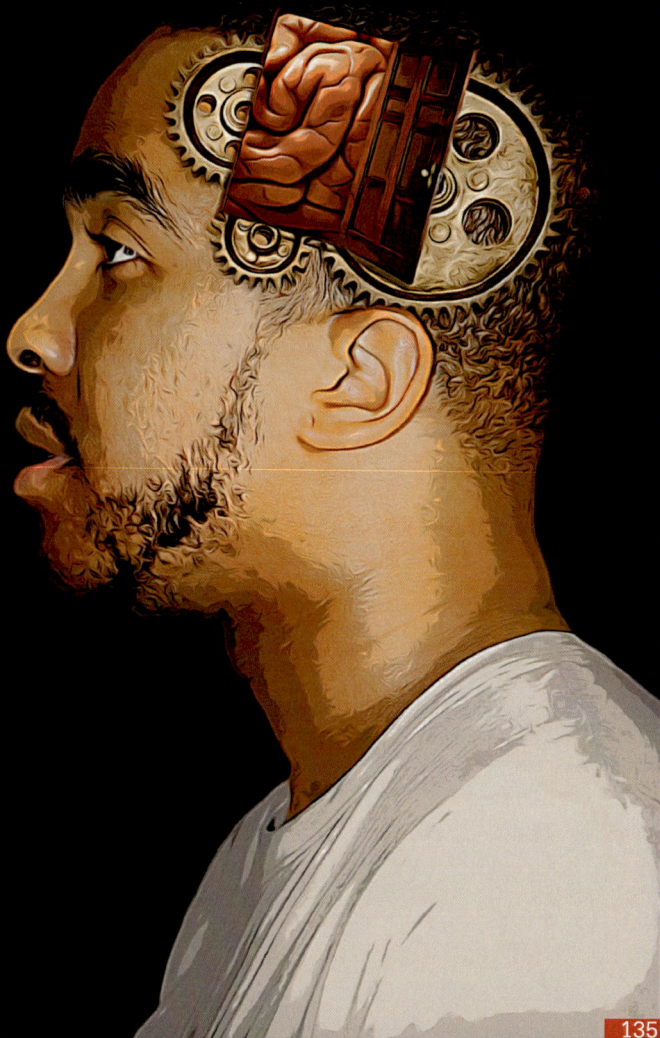

Come On In ;

And See

Why I

Hadn't.

3KP Marketing

After feeling like superman in and out of the bedroom, I believed lasting longer during oral and vaginal sex was all I needed to do, and that I was completely satisfying a woman when I went round for round. I was wrong!

I soon realized that I was not getting the reaction I wanted out of the women I were having sex with the kind of reaction the guys on adult sex tapes (like the ones found in my grandparents' room) were getting out of the women they were having sex with. I was copying the actions of those men and failing terribly. I was failing because I did not know the science of pleasing a woman until she had an orgasm. I would go round after round with some women and they would still not have an orgasm.

During sex, it was all about me feeling good; if she had an orgasm, she had one, and if she didn't, she just didn't. Even when I performed oral sex, I would just do it for a little while to get aroused. I was self-ish when it came to oral and vaginal sex because I did not know the science of sexually satisfying a woman. It was all about me. Because I did not know the science of sex and was only pleasing myself during sex for the most part, I came to the conclusion that I was not having sex with a woman...I was having sex with myself. I was only ejaculating inside of her. I strengthened my mind, self-esteem, and confidence, boosted my endurance, learned to breathe properly, and ate better food just so I could masturbate longer inside of her.

I know what you are thinking: you are thinking, how are you masturbating if you are having oral and vaginal sex, right?

Well when you think of masturbating, it's pleasing yourself sexually, right? You are stimulating your clitoris if you are a female and your penis if you are a male, until satisfaction has been met and you reach an orgasm. When I was having oral and vaginal sex, I was only focused on the stimulation of my penis (just as I would when I masturbated) and not the stimulation of the clitoris of the women I was having sex with. There were times I would stimulate the clitoris during vaginal sex, leading them to an orgasm (unnaturally) in the process of reaching an orgasm of my own depending on the position I was in during sex. I did not know how to naturally bring them to sexual satisfaction.

Soon after discovering that I had only been ejaculating inside of the women I had sex with, I discovered the science of how to satisfy women sexually; I had to stimulate the clitoris orally and through vaginal penetration exactly how my penis is stimulated during sex. **If I am not stimulating her clitoris, then I am not having sex with her. I am having sex with myself.**

After reflecting on my sexual encounters, I realized that women of color are taught at a very young age how to satisfy a man, and men of color are not taught how to satisfy a woman. Girls are drilled by the women in their family and subconsciously through music artists, actors, and actresses, to wear their hair, clothes, shoes and makeup a certain way, and to cook and clean so they can attract and keep a boyfriend and husband when they become of age.

When many girls reach the age where they are fertile and having sex, they learn how to satisfy the penis of a male orally, vaginally, and some through anal, by focusing on the male's reactions (body language) as they are stimulating his penis. Ever since they were a young girl, they are trained psychologically to appeal to and please men, not themselves. We are taught to focus on sports and to develop our talents so that we can become great and make a lot of money in life, not to attract and care for women when we grow up. When we become of age to begin dating, we are taught to attract girls with our gifts and talents, and by the size of our wallet. We are not taught how to appeal to them, to focus on their wellbeing, or to stimulate their clitoris, just please ourselves, therefore making us selfish during sex.

Many men both young and older believe women are satisfied because the woman they are with keep having sex with him. There are many women who fake sexual pleasure just to please their male partner, out of fear of him leaving her for another woman. I only mimicked the behaviors of the guys on the pornography tapes and those tapes did not teach the science of pleasing a woman. I wish they had, because some of the women I had sex with had to fake sexual satisfaction.

Because women of color have been taught how to care for men and how to stimulate the male penis, and many guys have not been taught how to care for a woman and stimulate the clitoris of a woman, many women believe sex is only for the pleasure of a man and they aren't supposed to reach a level of satisfaction during sex. And many men believe sex is for their own pleasure like I once believed.

What A Selfish Dick I Was!

Since there are many women in the world carrying the belief that sex is only for men, there are many women in the world who have never had an orgasm. I believe they all deserve to have plenty of them a couple every day, if they can.

JP Films

141

Women of color say and do many things to get me aroused: speak to me in a flirtatious manner, show their highest level of respect and appreciation for me, wearing their hair in certain styles (like a natural bob and silk press), wearing certain kind of dresses (like a maxi sundress), and walking a certain kind of way. Nurturing their kids, respecting other women no matter their background, age, or skin tone—sending nude selfies, or selfies in their underwear, cooking bottomless, rubbing my head after a fresh haircut, being seductive, telling me all the sexual things they wish to do to me, and much more. Women have a way of getting me ready for an orgasm without necessarily having to be in my presence. After learning the science of sexually satisfying a woman, I had to learn how to turn a woman on before the bedroom. Women of color taught me that foreplay started way before the bedroom.

Verdi Photography

I learned foreplay by investing a lot of time in women of color: listening to their conversations while they were getting their hair and nails done, talking on the phone at work or in public places, and by paying attention to things they shared on social media to name a few. Things they disliked about the guys they were involved with and complained to their girlfriends and shared on social media, were the behaviors I perfected and used to enhance my level of foreplay.

For example; women dislike lazy, disrespectful, irresponsible, emotionally unavailable, selfish, and unsuccessful men who have no sense of humor, which are the main things women complain to their girlfriends about and share to their social media accounts. I became more active and energetic, developed a high level of respect and a sense of humor for women and others, became very responsible and attentive to their needs and desires, I developed effective communication skills, and became selfless, all while continuing to achieve my goals and dreams. Subconsciously, these skills and behavior traits gave me an advantage over guys who do not invest in themselves or in women, and they helped me stimulate the mind, body, and spirit of a woman prior to touch.

My interpersonal skills, my play on words rather verbal or written, my high level of confidence, self-esteem, intelligence, energy, good hygiene, good eating habits, self-sufficiency, and knowing the science of satisfying a woman, have promoted me from being a minute man, to a master of seduction—creating magic and fireworks **In Between The Sheets: the real Magic Kingdom.**

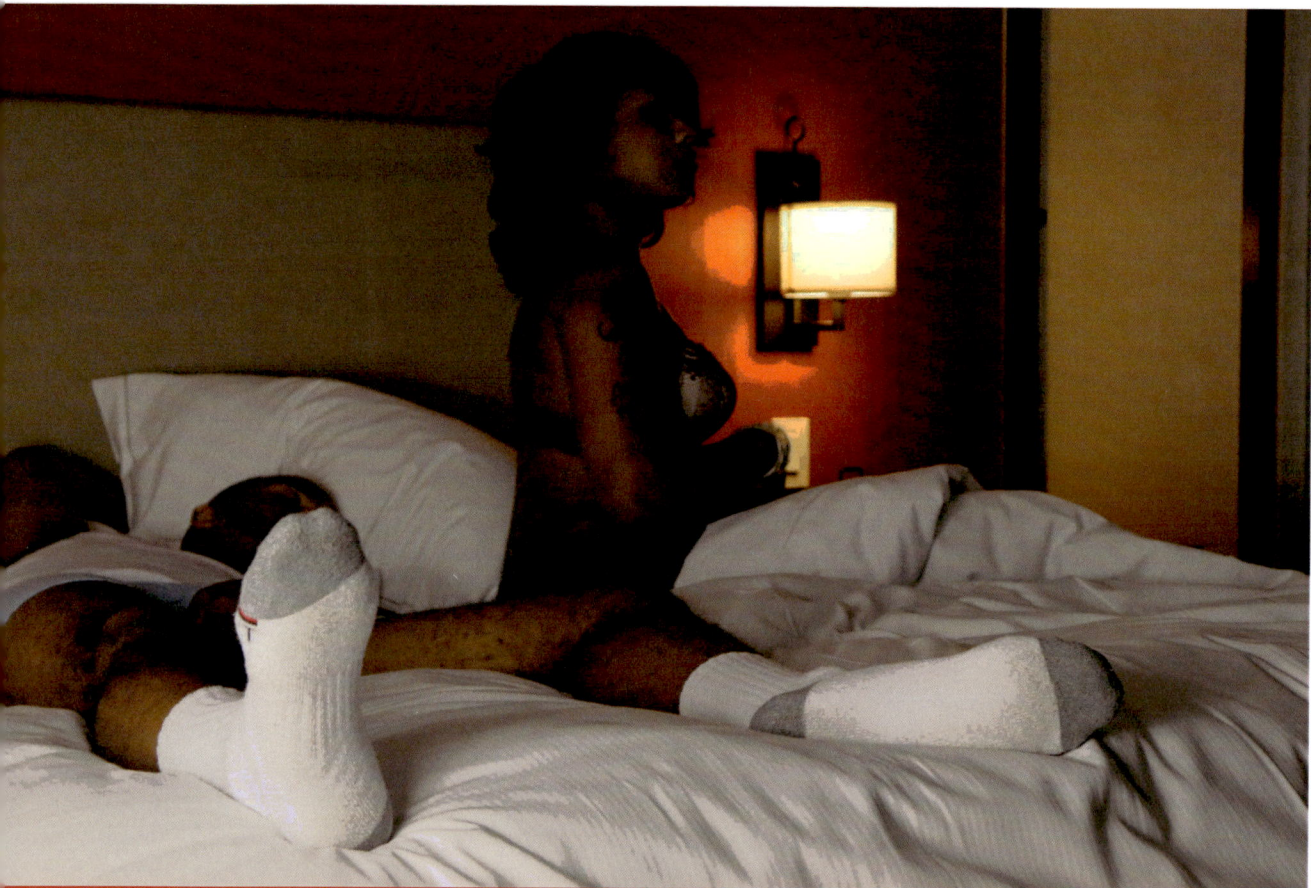

JP Films

You Don't Believe Me? Well Come On In And See

I'm in no race or competition to prove who can serve you better. I'm just here to let you know my touch is strictly reserved for me.

See, sex is a form of art and I am a gestural abstraction and graffiti artist. I am the brush to your canvas and the spray paint to your river mural. Once I insert my brush into your palette of paint, my only desire is to complete your portrait—spontaneously dribbling, splashing, and smearing your paint, while gliding my body onto your canvas until satisfaction has been reached.

I AM NOT HERE TO JUST WET MY BRUSH.

This spray can of mine will turn your walls into breathtaking waterfalls that you and I would often want to visit, like Niagara.

See, not only is the touch of my brush magical, so is my timing and affection. As you enjoy the thrill of me being with and inside you, I will be checking your vitals to breath at the same rate as you, to gasp and moan with you.

During our breathing intervals, I will be passionately licking, sucking, and kissing all on your sternocleidomastoid, breasts, and lips, along with each stroke of my brush until you begin to lose control and erupt.

As you are covering me with your April showers, I will be looking at you with excitement, deeply into your eyes, smiling at your expressions of satisfaction.

Wow! Look at my work.

You will be my canvas, and at this point you will be secured on my easel; no getting free. The strokes of my brush will begin to flow rapidly, increasing the rate of our simultaneously beating hearts.

Our synch gasps and moans will become more and more intense, as I time your next eruption to erupt with you, creating a very valuable work of art.

A FAMOUS PORTRAIT WILL BE MADE.

I want to create another one right after.

Only this time, you be the painter.

Dip my brush into your cup of water, then into your palette of paint, and begin softly stroking the bristles onto your blank canvas.

Turn your dry canvas into a magical waterfall when you submerge my brush deeper into your sparkling blue.

Paint a picture of a river flowing beautifully in the horizon.

Before I had you secured on my easel...now secure my easel in you and keep me near you until your portrait is complete. When you release your grip, I will know that magic and fireworks have been made again, in my **Magic Kingdom.**

So yes, It Is Worth It, You Can Work It. Put Your Thing Down, Flip It and Reverse It. lol.

Let's get **Completely Naked.**

CHAPTER FIVE

"MY CAKE & EATING IT TOO"

I apologize in advance, but the American Dream of being married with children and having a white picket fence is not a dream of mine. Will it ever be? More than likely not. With the exception of having children (because I already have a son), but I am not able to produce anymore. If you recall my story in Chapter One, my son was born when I was twenty-two years old and his mother and I did not plan to have him. To prevent bringing more children I would not be able to properly care for in this world, I went to my urologist and had him perform a vasectomy (cutting or blocking two tubes called the vas deferens so that sperm can no longer get into my semen) when I was twenty-four years old. My son was two years old at the time. The procedure was done during the time I was still involved with women who were broken, who had children of their own, and who were being very ugly towards the men who were trying to be fathers to their children, and before I was the successful man I am today.

While battling the demons and traumas I was facing during that time, I did not want to bring any more children into this world. I was incomplete as a man, trying to figure out and navigate this world, and still learning how to be a father to my son. Being as observant as I was to my behaviors, feelings, and surroundings back then, I have seen how many of the oldest children in most black families were neglected, while the middle and youngest children were receiving the attention, affection, love, and proper care from one or both parents. Older children suffer the most and often in silence, while fighting for the love and affection from their parents.

I learned early on in life that every child has special needs and desires, and they need individual time with their parents. I also learned that if parents had many children, it would be almost impossible for them to distribute love, affection, and proper care equally to all of their children, while still trying to achieve goals and dreams of their own. I got a vasectomy because I did not want my son to experience neglect from his father because his father had an army of kids. I wanted to be accessible to his needs, wants and desires. Some may call it selfish; I call it making one of the best decisions I have ever made as a young adult man of color. I would rather have one child I can take care of fully, then have a million kids I cannot care for. There are many guys out here who are terrible fathers, and that was not going to be me. The amount of money good fathers have to pay in child support because they no longer want to be involved with the mother of their children is ridiculous.

Jaheir Davis

"I take care of the financial obligations for my child; you take my child away from me because I no longer want to be with you and because I do not want to be with you, I have to pay a percentage to the Child Support System (white men), in order for them to pay you for the pain I have caused you for leaving you. Money that my child may never see"

FUCK THAT! That shit does not feel good. It does NOT feel good at all.

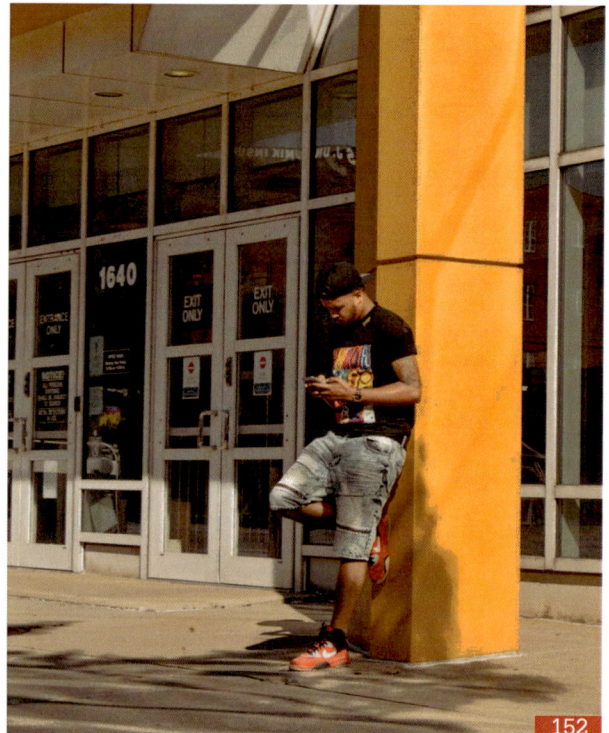

"I legally marry you and we decide to split up. Because we split up I have to pay the Domestic Relations Court (white men) a percentage of my earnings, to pay you for the pain and suffering you are experiencing because we agreed to split up.

FUCK THAT! That shit does not feel good. It does NOT feel good at all.

That is a trap I am definitely not trying to be trapped in. The American Dream is not mine. I do not trust white men, their systems of oppression, and women of color who use their systems to help destroy the lives of innocent and successful men of color.

Many people desire to have the American Dream but have no plan to make it happen just wishful thinking. I learned early on in life that **a goal without a plan is just a dream.** I had no concrete plan to achieve my desires, but I was not going to allow myself to get sucked into a vicious trap I have seen many people fall into because they made decisions based on emotions instead of intelligence, and because they did not take the time to plan properly.

I also learned to think for myself and to no longer allow other people, television, film, and music to influence my decisions or behavior, which most people tend to do. Most people get into relationships because they see people on social media, movies, and television in one not because of their own beliefs, values, and principles. After learning to think for myself, I realized that I do not need the government's permission to date, have sex with, care for, or to live with a woman, and I do not need their permission to marry one. If I was to be in a relationship with a woman, I would already be physically, mentally, emotional ly, and spiritually married to her until we decide to part ways; if a decision is made to part ways, we can do so without legal action.

I can marry the woman, but I cannot marry the system. For me, the only difference between a relationship and a legal marriage is: one you don't need permission from the courts to separate, and one you do...which often ends with a heavy balance owed. I am not telling people to not get legally married; it's just not on my radar, and I will not allow anyone to convince me otherwise.

Being in a relationship is not a priority of mine. My previous relationships happened because I desired to be in them, not because I needed to be in them. For the most part, the desire to be in relationships with those women came from their influence and outside influences (friends, family, social media, etc.) knowing I was not ready.

It is nice to be in the company of a woman who is no longer broken, but an intimate relationship is not a requirement for me to be happy or to achieve greater things in life. I have already found happiness within myself, so there is really nothing any woman can do to make me feel happy. What I do not like and will not tolerate is being in the company of a woman who does not value my perspectives and who attempts to change my mind about the American Dream wedding and family life.

"I am not for you and that is perfectly fine; I am for me and maybe someone else. Do not pressure me to conform to your way of life, instead invest your time and energy into someone who is ready to move in your direction. I am the perfect version of me and if that makes you unhappy, I am not sorry."

I am a very important component to society because I understand others; I consider their perspectives and empathize with them, including those from diverse backgrounds and cultures. Because I am strong minded and stand firmly on my beliefs, many women I come across do not care about my thoughts, feelings, and beliefs. All they seem to care about is them. Many are not socially aware and do not foster an environment of cultural respect, which is very important to me.

Until I reached my late twenties, I felt that my life was influenced and controlled by the thoughts and behaviors of others. I tried being in monogamous relationships because of the social influences of others, and they never worked out for me. Being in those relationships felt like I was limiting myself—being housed in a controlled environment with no opportunity to escape. Now that I am in my early thirties, it is my time to be free. Free to be me—and that does not mean inserting my lightning rod between the thighs of many different women, because I also have a strong sense of self-control and discipline. It means being free from limitations, fears, and other people's insecurities, thoughts and opinions of me. However, I really love double layered, German chocolate cake with coconut pecan frosting, but not every woman can bake it to my liking. So, I can't have my cake and eat it too.

I feel like the shackles have been lifted off of my potential since removing myself from past relationships where I felt I couldn't be myself. I enjoy the freedom to move gracefully as I please. Since freeing myself from those relationships, I learned I am my best when I am not limiting myself to someone else's expectations for me. I have achieved more successes as a single man than I have being with a woman. This does not mean that I am unable to achieve any successes with a woman in the future—because I am positive that I can with my discipline and skill set—but for now, I am just enjoying the breeze of emotional and mental freedom. With the feeling of someone blocking my potential removed, I am able to think,   create, and work better.

Although I am currently not in a relationship, I have an abundance of beautiful and amazing women friends who value and support my beliefs, differences,

and accomplishments. I am not alone, if you were wondering.

In terms of having sex: it is the way of life; it is human nature. Sex is an even exchange of energy and if a woman wishes to offer her body to me and I offer my body to her in return, I do not owe her anything extra. Fair exchange is no robbery. I have learned to separate the emotions of love from sex (which most people often confuse), and until I decide to give myself fully to a woman in the form of a relationship, I am not bound by any relationship terms and conditions, and therefore I belong to myself.

Until a woman decides to fully give herself to me in the form of a relationship, she is not bound by any terms and conditions either, and she belongs to herself. Even if we agree to establish a relationship together, we still belong to ourselves. I will not have control over her, and she will not have control over me. We shall work as a team, not as each other's parents. Love is spiriual and sex is biological. What we do with our bodies is our choice by divine right for we own ourselves. It's our decision if we decide to stay with a person if they share their body with another person, and as for me what a woman does with her body is her own business, as it's her body not mine. Her having sex with another man is not a deal breaker for me unless she does so carelessly - giving me something I can't get rid of like HIV and AIDS, or becoming conceived by another man. Love is spiritual and sex is biological. I don't associate love with sex, as many others do, especially women. I say this because, if you remove the penis you lose the woman, rather you deposit it in the womb of another woman, it malfunctions like I stated in "Minute Man," or you just are no longer sexually interested in her. Remove the penis and she will remove herself and all things attached to her. Sex is biological and love is spiritual. Without the sex, she loses the emotional attachment and the need to stick around - sex which she associates with love. Remove the penis and you lose the woman, unless she know the difference between love and sex.

" There should be no disappointment over love, and there would be nono if people understand the difference between love and sex. The major difference is that Love is spirital, while Sex is biological. Noe experience, which touches the human heart with a spiritual force, can possibly be harmful, except through ignorance jealousy."

"A Good Man who is Wrongfully Convicted will Lose his Woman to a Bum with a Working Penis and a Brother in the Military will Lose his Wife to his Brother or Best Friend with an Available Penis who Exhausted his Savings Account."

#CompletelyNaked

As for me, if the woman removes her vagina, my love and investment will still be present, for I am not ignorant to the difference between sex and love, and I am not jealous or envious of anyone. Although, I may not be sexually attracted to her, I still can be invested in her in many other ways until the desire to have sex with her returns and we agree to engage in sexual activity. I don't have to get rid of her for good, as love is law, family is business and sex is biological.

"A loving relationship is one in which the loved one is free to be himself, to laugh with me, but never at me; to cry with me, but never because of me; to love life, to love himself, and to love being loved. Such a relationship should be based upon freedom and can never grow in a jealous heart." -- **Leo F. Buscaglia**

Love is Natural. Love is Pure. Love is Priceless.
Love is Infinite. It is not limited, nor forced.
Love flows like the wind that blows leaves off trees.

Love is not vocal. It is not written words.
Love is a feeling of Happiness that people feel.

Love is an action and it departs when it knows
people do not appreciate it.

So either you learn to appreciate it or
let it go for someone else to cherish.

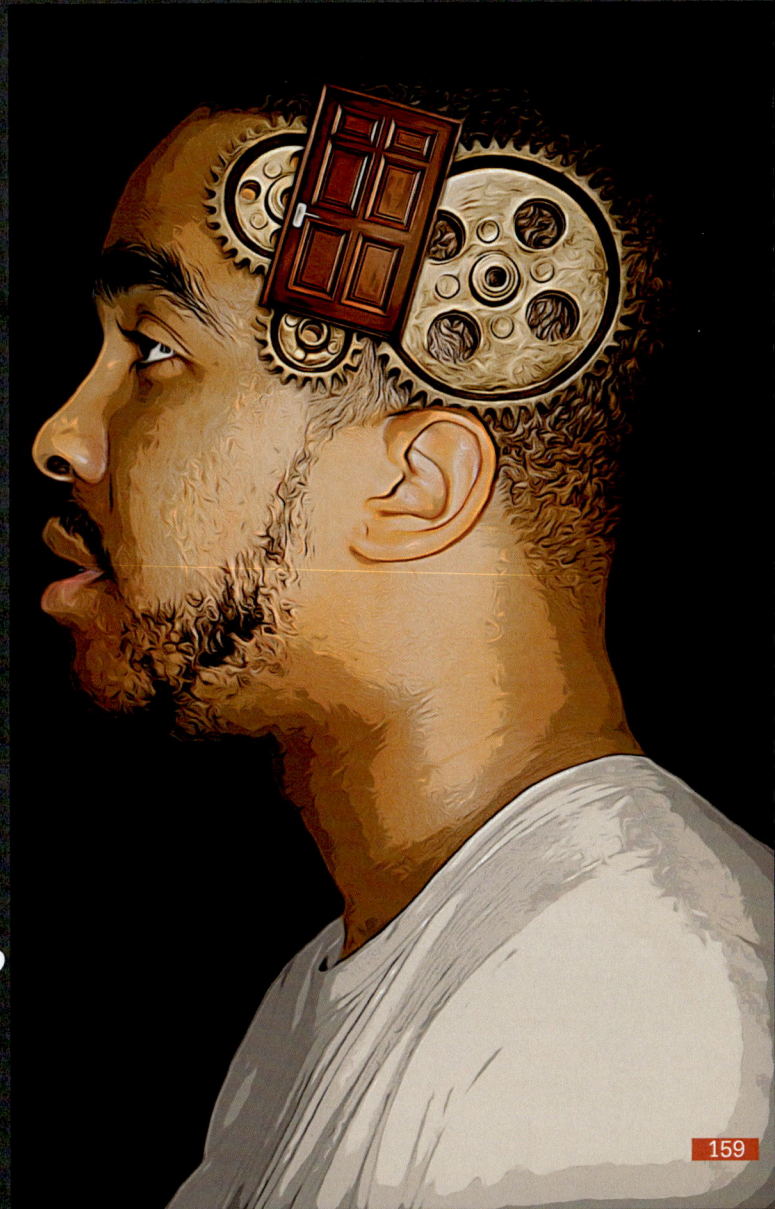

You Have Seen Me Completely Naked. Now, I Must Put My Clothes Back On.

3KP Marketing

It's very difficult to relax and enjoy life in a world that makes you stand guard — protecting your mind, body, spirit and the wellbeing of others because you are one of a kind. A world that makes you so tense.

But, through all of the toxic energy this world possess, that's distributed by people who are evil, who hate themselves as well as others[because their parents have never taught them what it means to Love Thyself and their teachers have never pointed them in the direction of securing themselves before securing a diploma/degree, and because they never cared for learning how to truly love themselves and others] Still I Stand!

I Stand as Me.

Not with my Back Against the World, but with the World Facing Me!

REMARKS FROM THE ATHOR

REMARKS FROM THE AUTHOR

One of the hardest obstacles I have ever had to face alone, but overcame was the obstacle of separating myself from who I want to be, from who the world thinks and wants me to be.

I overcame that obstacle by first suspending every thought someone had about me, both good and bad. Then, I removed myself from individuals who never allowed me to have a voice, who encouraged me to dance in my own degradation, as well as individuals who consciously and subconsciously attempted to exterminate my happiness.

While away, I invested fully into activities I enjoyed, and activities that challenged me for the better, in which I paid close attention to and documented via writing, my thoughts, feelings and emotions. Overtime, I developed the ability to ignore, one of my greatest abilities. I developed the ability to ignore the negative influences of other people, those which are attracted to and adopted by those who lack discipline, which leads to the destruction of oneself and others. With the discipline to ignore outside negative forces, I have learned to think on my own and challenge those who take on the role of Education using my impulse voice; not the voice of my parents, not the voice of the elders, or the voice of tradition, or the establishment. But my own voice.

Within a short period of time, I freed myself from who everyone else wanted me to be and became myself.

Now that I am found, there are still many people who work diligently in an attempt to throw me off track and who are upset because I do not operate on their level of vibrations, and because I do not conform to society's standards of how to live; love, foster relationships, succeed, and so forth, as they have done. As I mentioned in my second book, Cultivating Minds To Own Thyself, "If I lived my life doing only what you approved of me to do, I wouldn't be me."

Negative people hate positive people, and such people should not have access to your mind, which is your most powerful asset. If they have your mind, then they have you. If you keep your mind, then you keep you. This is how I was able to overcome the obstacle of separating who I want to be, from who the world thinks and wants me to be.

I have also dedicated Completely Naked to the many people I have harmed as a result of the psychic trauma I have endured from the forefathers of Chattel Slavery and their families who keep the cycle of oppression spinning on what seems to be a never-ending axis. This book is also written for the millions of people who are still affected by the horrific conditions, and those people who are not of color and who seem to not be affected by the conditions of our enslavement.

After revealing my truth to the world, I learned that keeping my emotions and the things that bothered me inside made me weak and less of a man, because it affected my behavior and relationships with others. I felt I was being eaten alive. Releasing my anger and frustration and sharing my experiences with others in a positive way made me stronger. Getting Completely Naked helped shape me into the man I am today.

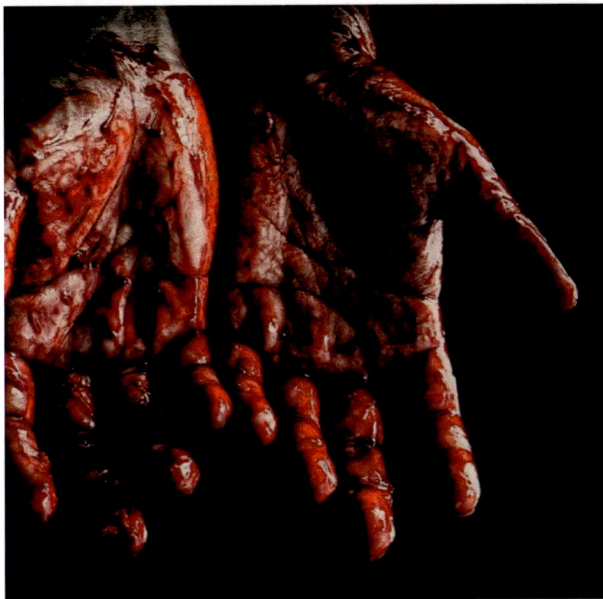

Blood isn't pleasant at all; but many of us have blood on our hands and don't even know it."

WHO HURT YOU?

I wish I had a permanent healing bandage for those who have long been at war with those who have caused them a great deal of pain.

The damage they have caused is not pretty at all and the way many of you treat yourselves and others as a result of the pain that you have endured, isn't right at all. You are hurting and you want people to feel what you are feeling because you are hurt?

I wish I could set you free.

Your fight isn't with people who haven't caused you pain, your war is with your enemies, your war is with yourself! — Get Right Within! Get Right With Them! Set those hostages, who've done you no harm, free from your prison. Harming them will only cause you to hurt more.

"TEARS OF A HUMMINGBIRD"

Tears of a Hummingbird
A Novel by NeeNee Marie

Could You Fly with A Broken Wing?

The dark tragedies from her childhood have followed her into her adult life like déjà vu.

Symone Baker-Michaels, a delicate, yet strong Black woman finds it nearly impossible to obtain freedom as she remains locked down and struggles to break free from the shackles of abuse. Somehow, she seeks out a slither of hope and finds inner strength to fight for her life...

literally. Symone digs deep inside of herself to battle against generational- curses, with aim to end the cycle of misery for good. But at what expense? What will Symone have to sacrifice before she can cross over to a life of healing and peace, rather than pain and suffering? Who will she have to give up before her spirit is able to fly freely... or will she ever fly again at all?

NEENEE MARIE

Tears
Of A
Hummingbird

It's Nobody's Job To Fix You.
It's Your Job To Fix You!

You can only put yourself back together!

—

No one is required to give you their all because you had it bad.
Get rid of the attitude that "someone owes you something because
you are broken," because even if they tried to give themselves to you,
you will harm them with your sharp edges. Now, there are two damaged people.

How will you help them heal and you are the piece that pierced their
major artery?

World Attention & Validation Will Not Heal Your Wounds.
You Need Self-Love: A Surgery Only You Can Perform.

That sexual pleasure he or she is giving you in your broken
state is only numbing cream. That excruciating pain will be
on its way back soon.

You Need Surgery.

PLAN OF ACTION

Sisters, I am requesting your assistance in helping me undress the men in your life—who are experiencing mental pain caused by trauma—overcome their pain and trauma by purchasing or encouraging them to purchase a copy of this book. I need you to begin a discussion with them, encouraging them to open up on the topics enclosed in this book. Please do not pressure them to answer or overwhelm them with your questions, just allow them to open up naturally. Be patient and empathetic. When you ask certain questions, give your reasons for asking; be sure to let them know you are not asking questions to trigger them, but are asking because you care about their mental health, and so they can release their bottled up anger and frustration safely with you, so they can begin to heal properly. No more suffering in silence.

The more men we can get to read and discuss this book, the more men we can help return to their natural (unbroken) state, therefore helping our women cut the locks off and remove the chains from their psychologically independent (broken) mind, allowing us to fully love ourselves and one another.

How Success Became My Focus

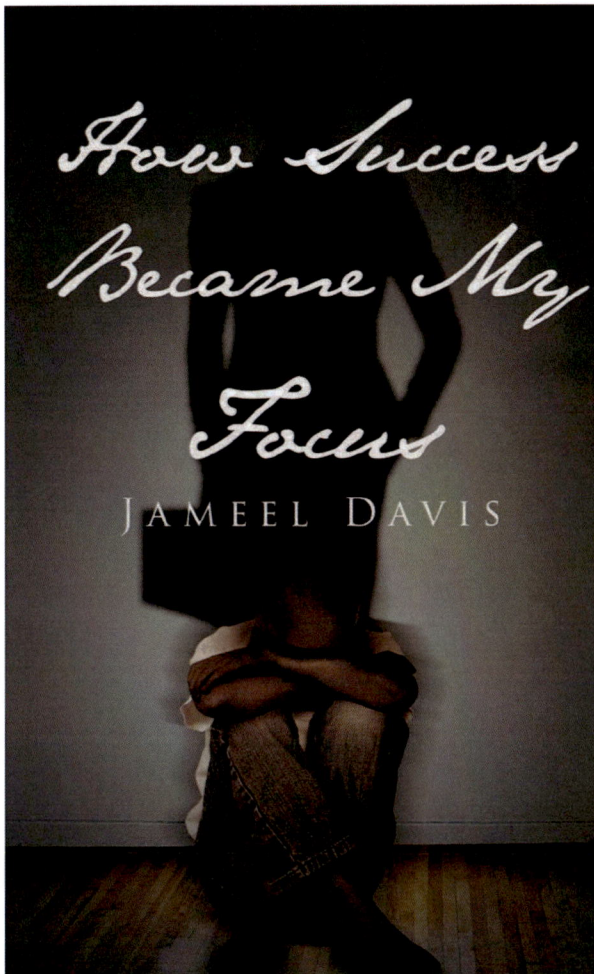

Have you ever felt so lost in life that you don't know where you are heading to? Do you ever feel like giving up even after you've given your all? Does it seem like your best isn't just enough? Well, worry no more. Set aside your anxieties, be inspired, and reach greater heights with How Success Became My Focus.

With enthusiasm, Jameel Davis will stir your passion and divert your energies toward determination as he shares his success story. He overcame his struggles and emerged from being an ordinary student to a successful and respectable individual that he is now. Geared toward success, Davis was able to motivate himself to stand out from others and better himself. He steered his life around and directed his momentum to the path that aided him to rise from his downfall. Despite life's pitfalls, Davis was able to conquer it all through his willpower. So if ever you feel down and discouraged, never lose hope. Always remember that there is more to life. Come out from your shell like Davis did and-be an inspiration to others. Go out, inspire, and stand out with How Success Became My Focus.

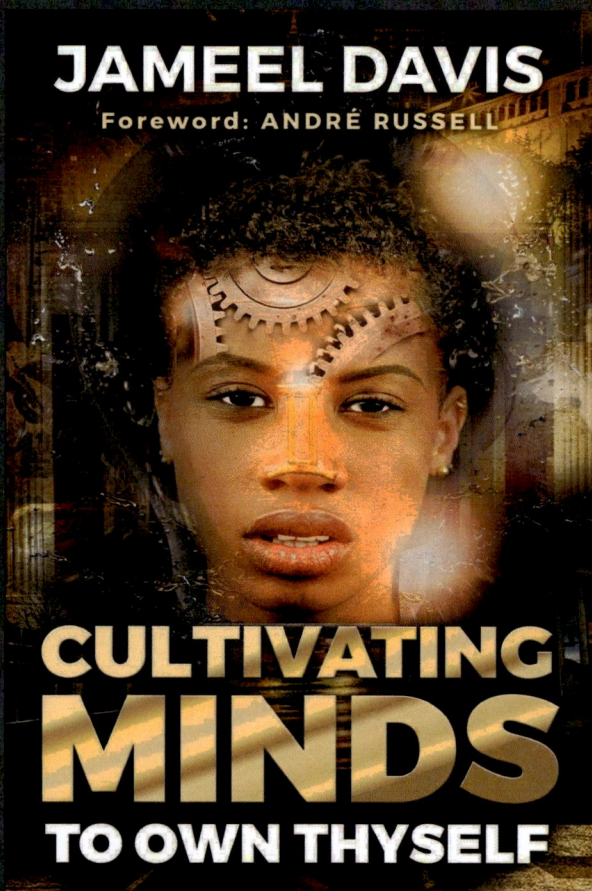

JAMEEL DAVIS

Foreword: ANDRÉ RUSSELL

CULTIVATING MINDS TO OWN THYSELF

Cultivating Minds To Own Thyself

Cultivating Minds To Own Thyself was birthed with the intentions of helping men and women discover their purpose and to take ownership of their life without using society's standards. It teaches readers how to examine themselves in an attempt to modify their thoughts and in turn become their best self as well as make a difference in the lives of others.

Davis' tale outlines what it takes to overcome having a false identity and being miseducated and conditioned by society's norm.

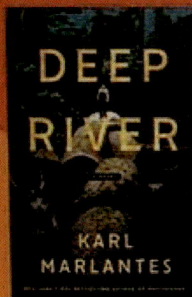

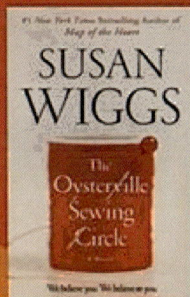

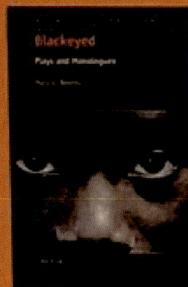

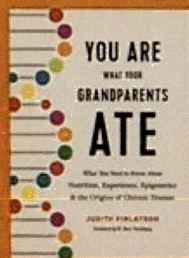

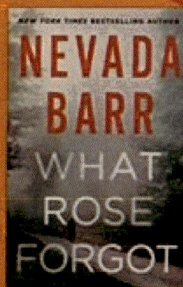

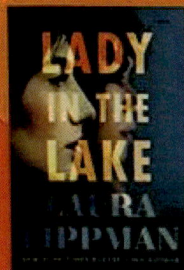

In Between These Sheets

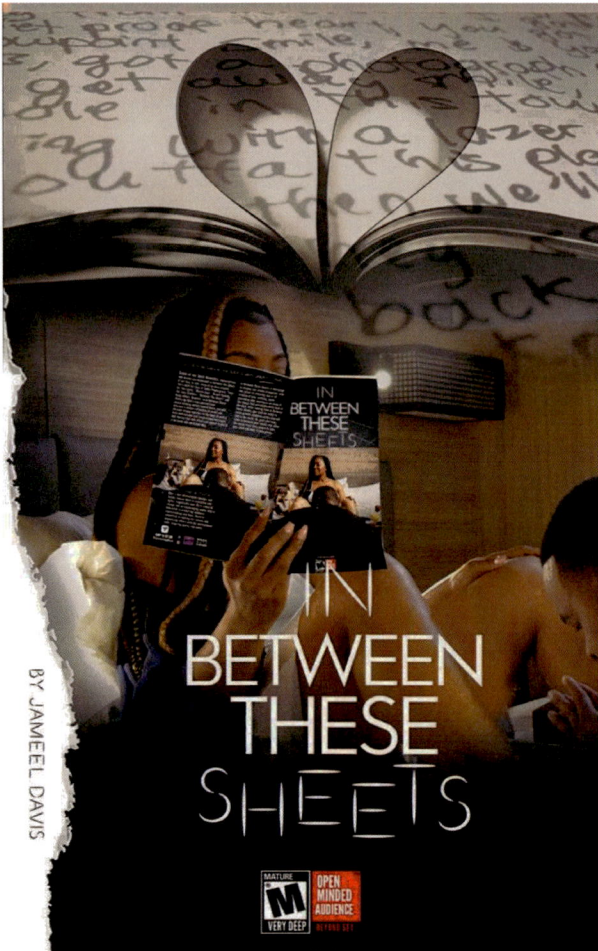

Some of our best moments, conversations and dreams are developed in between the sheets of our bed. In fact, many of us were created there with the help of Teddy Pendergrass, "Turn Off The Lights," Marvin Gaye, "Sexual Healing," the Isley Brothers, "Between The Sheets" and many others. However, in In Between These Sheets by Cleve-land Author Jameel Davis, you will discover a unique collection of words and phrases strung together in the form of poetry, both motivational and inspirational messages, and stories that will affect and appeal to you in a personal and emotional way.

In Between These Sheets is dedicated to helping you create mindgasms with the option of removing any or all articles of your clothing, while expanding your awareness on many of the things that are deliberately kept in the dark. After coming from In Between These Sheets, you shall be ready to reach greater climaxes within yourself and in the world.

So, grab your wine, slide in between your sheets and allow the words from these pages to take your mind and body to new places.

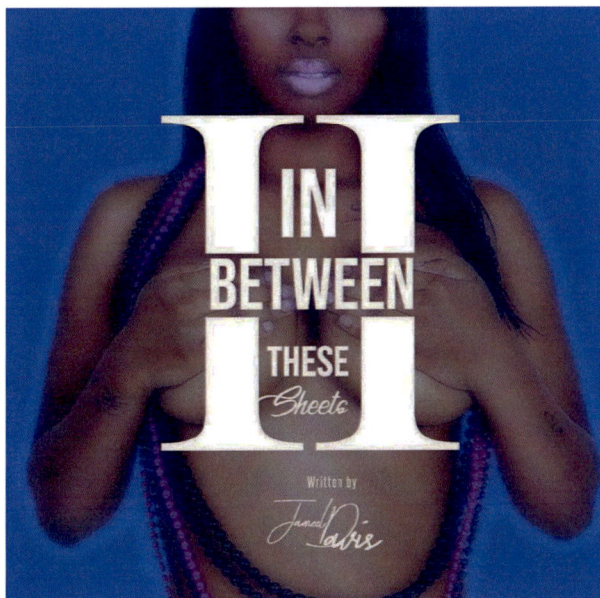

IN BETWEEN THESE SHEETS II COMING SOON...

Sex is very beautiful and artistic in nature. The vibrant colors, creativity and excitement it produces when mixed together properly, safely, and respectfully with someone special who loves painting our blank canvases with nasty sex and intensifying orgasms as much as me, are moments worth living for. And, I am certain you love and crave those moments of ecstasy as well.

Here, I have spilled colorful paints of sex on these sheets for your enjoyment, that is guaranteed to boost your sex-esteem. So, unleash your purring housecat from your panties and let her run wild in between these sheets with you.

You want it and I wanted you to want it. Now turn it on over, open it up and press your face down into the sheets as I dig deep into the soul of your cat, making her juicy for the both of us.

Enjoy this Erotic Memoir and collection of erotic stories by Cleveland Author Jameel Davis

No cats were harmed during the making of this book.

Chapter 1: I Cheated

All broken people who are in a relationship with someone cheat, entertain the thought of cheating and will eventually cheat

Chapter 1: I Cheated

Women Love Men Who Cheat!
UNTIL THEY ARE THE ONES BEING CHEATED ON

Chapter 2: Finding the Love of a Black Man

If you do not think highly of yourself or feel great about yourself, you aren't able to receive the love others are giving you because you do not have love for yourself. In fact, you aren't able to achieve your desires and operate at your fullest potential.

Because you do not see yourself in the highest light, do not feel complete within, and because you are not able to recognize and receive the love someone is giving you, your personal insecurities, self-doubt, and low self-esteem serves as a deterrent to the love and blessings that are trying to come your way. You are pushing it all away.

You cannot expect anyone to love you or mention they do not love you, or expect to receive blessings if you do not know what love looks or feels like.

You should not be dating or be involved with anyone until you see yourself in the highest light and feel great about your entire being because you are going to run a good person away by beating on yourself.

If you are expecting someone to fill a void that only you can fill, they are going to fall short every time which will cause you to become upset and angry, driving them away.

Take time out and learn you. Spend time alone ignoring the voices of your parents, of the community, of the establishment and embrace who you were created to be.

Practice speaking highly of yourself, hugging yourself, dancing with yourself, singing to yourself, challenging yourself and going on adventures by yourself. This is how you will develop self-love, receive your desires and how you will be able to recognize and receive love from others.

Chapter 5: My Cake & Eating It Too

That ring you bought her won't heal the pain
her daddy has caused her; she's married to pain and
she's still hungry for attention and affection from other men.

You aren't enough.

Her ring attracts them when you are away,
she allows them inside of her.

Chapter 5: My Cake & Eating It Too

She hasn't posted her ring after the wedding
she desperately wanted to have, that you weren't ready for.
Her body screams she's available to other men, while her
mind screams you are her husband.
She is poison.

Chapter 5: My Cake & Eating It Too

That ring won't stop him from cheating;
he proposed to you on a broken knee, in his broken state
and your broken heart accepted his proposal to hurt you
till death do you part.

Nothing lasts forever and everything is temporary:
because of that, I don't expect tenderness, love and happiness
to always be present.
I don't expect to not get hurt or to not feel aching pain.
I don't expect people to always be around or to show up when it
counts, because it's bound to not happen.

The only thing I expect is
me finding peace within myself when feelings that feel good fade
away, as a result of the evilness the world has instilled in people.
I owe that to myself.

*"THE GOOD NEVER OUTWEIGHS THE BAD IN THE MAJORITY
OF MOST PEOPLE MIND."*

One small hiccup can erase ten-years of beautiful memories,   successful accomplishments and well established relationships — permanently staining lifelong grudges and resentment on the minds of those who were affected.

However, in my mind your bad never really matters, if you live tomorrow making your bad good, your good better, and your better best.

That is what separates me from the majority — Your Good Outweighs Your Bad Always, when you invest into a brighter tomorrow.

OPEN YOUR CELLPHONE CAMERA,
SCAN THE CODE BELOW, CLICK THE LINK
AND FOLLOW ME ON INSTAGRAM

CULTIVATINGMINDS_

www.ingramcontent.com/pod-product-compliance
Lightning Source LLC
Chambersburg PA
CBRC091801090426
42811CB00021B/1904